STEPPING STONES
—— TO ——
PERSONAL HEALING

A Traditional Physician Goes
Beyond the Limitations of
His Medical Background
and Embraces the World
of Holistic Health.

ROBERT N KOPPEN MD

BALBOA.
PRESS

A DIVISION OF HAY HOUSE

Balboa Press books may be ordered through booksellers or by contacting:

Balboa Press
A Division of Hay House
1663 Liberty Drive
Bloomington, IN 47403
www.balboapress.com
1 (877) 407-4847

Because of the dynamic nature of the Internet, any web addresses or
links contained in this book may have changed since publication and
may no longer be valid. The views expressed in this work are solely those
of the author and do not necessarily reflect the views of the publisher,
and the publisher hereby disclaims any responsibility for them.

The author of this book does not dispense medical advice or prescribe the use
of any technique as a form of treatment for physical, emotional, or medical
problems without the advice of a physician, either directly or indirectly. The
intent of the author is only to offer information of a general nature to help
you in your quest for emotional and spiritual well-being. In the event you use
any of the information in this book for yourself, which is your constitutional
right, the author and the publisher assume no responsibility for your actions.

Any people depicted in stock imagery provided by Thinkstock are
models, and such images are being used for illustrative purposes only.
Certain stock imagery © Thinkstock.

Print information available on the last page.

ISBN: 978-1-5043-8020-1 (sc)
ISBN: 978-1-5043-8022-5 (e)

Library of Congress Control Number: 2017907381

Balboa Press rev. date: 07/18/2017

This book was first published in 1995.

Stepping Stones is an important read for those who desire to be in charge of their own health and healing.

Dr. Robert Koppen skillfully leads the reader through the mind-body connection, methodically revealing its ability to create health or disease.

Based on his decades of practice, Dr.Koppen makes this subject approachable and understandable, empowering the reader to take action.

—**Janine Wilburn**
Founder
Touch.Nology Holdings LLC
San Francisco, California

Compellingly pragmatic, Stepping Stones elucidates some of the most vexing mind-body health issues. Dr. Koppen promotes a bona fide medical breakthrough through his approach to physical and mental problems. By outlining ways in which his patients successfully restored hope through self-reliance, his unique perspective presents a doorway to understanding health and spirit to anyone ready to reclaim their lives from the medical pharmaceutical spider web. I highly recommend this brief, yet clear gem to all my students and patients.

—**Danielle Godfrey**
Certified Yoga Instructor
Phoenix, Arizona

Dr. Robert Koppen, a deeply insightful and truly compassionate man of healing, has produced this gem of wisdom and humor for us all. How fortunate that book and reader have found each other.

—Rabbi Michael Shapiro
Phoenix, Arizona

This book contains a wealth of spiritual information. It is a helpful guide to the perplexities of life. Dr. Robert Koppen, former surgeon and now transformational counselor and healer, has been able to transmit universal principles by means of case histories taken from his own practice. An important addition for those attempting to make meaningful changes in their lives.

—Abram Ber, MD
Homeopathic Physician
Scottsdale, Arizona

As a professional singer of forty years, in 2008 I was diagnosed with follicular thyroid cancer. Afraid for my life, and of losing my singing voice, I became committed to both my complete emotional and physical healing as well as understanding why my body was expressing disease. It was this search that lead me to Dr. Robert Koppen and his book *"Stepping Stones To Personal Healing"*. In his book, Dr. Koppen shares both his personal and professional experiences, offering suggestive help for those seeking answers to troubles of the mind, body and spirit. With his medical and spiritual guidance (as shared in his book) Dr. Koppen helped me release and clear past and present life trauma allowing me to forgive those situations, in turn helping me to discover a healthy and new spiritual consciousness within myself. "Stepping Stones" gifts it's reader a gentle, non invasive approach to the spiritual principles of holistic and energetic medicine as well as an alternative to healing with or without the need for conventional medicine. This loving book is a must for anyone seeking to attain and maintain complete health.

—Janene Lovullo
Orange County, California

Dr. Robert Koppen's book *"Stepping Stones To Personal Healing"* is a profound tool and exceptional book that provides a simple instrument to people from all backgrounds to heal and teach themselves self empowerment. It is the answer to heal and cope with many of the modern day challenges faced.

I highly recommend this special book; it truly is a wonderful comprehensive approach to profound healing and happiness. It is my sincere pleasure to have known and worked with Dr. Koppen for many years. he has been and continues to be an integral asset to me and my patients.

—Paul Stallone, NMD
Scottsdale, Arizona

Dr. Koppen has a wealth of knowledge and is a wonderful person. This comes through in his book Stepping Stones. In it he shares his wisdom and understanding of how strong the connection is between our emotions and the resulting physical manifestations in our bodies. I found the chapter on allergies and not feeling safe in the world especially helpful as well as the techniques for healing. Dr. Koppen and his book have been a blessing to my life and my family!

—Amy Vance
Scottsdale, Arizona

With one foot in front of the other and the Stepping Stones workbook, anyone truly seeking health in their life can succeed. Each chapter of Stepping Stones presents a complete message, and can be read at random or sequentially, allowing the reader to walk away after a mere 5 minutes with a new outlook on healing.

Dr. Koppen includes numerous stories collected from his own practice which inspired me to draw connections between my own physical, emotional, and spiritual selves. But mostly, I awakened deeper to the limitless power of love. This book will contribute to my work as a soul-inspired coach and trainer, as well as to the lives of those who journey step by step toward a clearer sense of well being.

—Joy Taylor
Soul-Inspired Life Coach
Mt. Shasta, California

"Dr. Robert N. Koppen draws upon his own experiences as a physician and a spiritual healer/guide to bring together this unique compilation of articles about personal healing. These articles are filled with insights and recommendations that provide the reader with a more comprehensive approach to health/wellness. He cites many different examples and brings together not only his own personal experiences but those of his patients to get a better understanding of the underlining causes of illness. He illustrates how our feelings and emotions affect not only the physical body, but also the environment around us. Dr. Koppen shares a deep understanding of the body-mind-spirit connection. A beautiful reminder of our own divine connection. He also provides the reader with useful tools to bring about changes and inspires us to take personal responsibility for our own inner healing."

—Marin Lutz
Topanga, California

Ten years ago, I read Stepping Stones, and found it to be interesting and thought provoking. Recently, I re-read Stepping Stone and found it to be profound and accurate. What a difference ten years makes! My spiritual and healthy-living has led me to know, experience, and confirm the ideas presented in Dr. Koppen's book. His understanding of the connections among our physical-emotional-spiritual bodies provides an effective, natural healing approach to caring for ourselves. His guidance allows us to heal our physical bodies and grow spirituality. I'm so grateful for your guidance, Dr. Koppen.

—Diane Hughes, MEd
Spiritually-Guided Energy Practitioner
Tempe, Arizona

An outstanding collection of articles that have appeared in publications across the country, including Arizona Networking News. Subjects range from general health to the consequences of a judgmental attitude and how our mind creates the state of health or illness which our body experiences. All have deeply meaningful spiritual teachings.

—Arizona Networking News
December 1995 issue

Dr. Koppen has written a timeless and significant book on the multi-dimensional aspects of healing.

He communicates his journey openly and authentically, and gives the reader "doses" of brief chapters on crucial health issues with examples, spiritual wisdom and practical steps.

For example, in Chapters 3 ("Rejuvenation") and 7("Allergies"), Dr. Koppen gives a simple, clear overview of the health issue and offers & practical steps which can be applied to one's wholeness healing and quality of life.

Intertwined throughout this gem of a book is the reminder of our true Source of healing and of our essential Divine nature.

—A. Mattison
Larkspur, California

Attitude adjustments! Illuminations! Insights! A clearly spoken, nearly simple, to-the-point read. Empowering. Mind-altering. Life-altering. Health-altering. Healing.

Read and hear Dr. Koppen's keen observations connecting the physical experience to spiritual understandings, and practice his suggestions. Use the workbook-type pages for your notes, ideas and personal work. Highly recommended. Many opportunities for critical personal growth are at hand in this focused and highly inspired slim volume. Pick it up often and scan again for new adjustment points. Share and discuss to expand the positivity in your world and the world at large. Dr. Koppen interprets life now as calling us to our Higher, Healing Selves!

Rich material for humans on earth at this time, connecting the dots of one's life to expand forward movement. Excellent!

—Nimueh Rephael
Phoenix, Arizona

DEDICATION

*This book is dedicated to those of us
who are now willing to learn and apply
in their daily lives
more of the spiritual
teachings that have
always been available
to us but which we have
chosen to ignore until now.*

ACKNOWLEDGEMENTS

*This book could not have been put
together without the help
from the following human divine instruments:*

My beloved late wife, *Joan,* for helping
me to create the undisturbed
space in which these articles could be written
and for typing them up faithfully;

Jackie Pieters, editor of the former
Arizona Light newspaper, and
Joanne Henning Tedesco, editor of
the Arizona Networking News,
for their regular stimulation to produce more articles;

Dr. Abram Ber, for his encouragement about
the quality of these articles;

Rabbi Michael Shapiro, for handing me some of the
spiritual themes and ideas that I used;

Helene Harris, for helping me to realize that a
collection of 30 articles is already a book;

Kristin Haraldson Goldenthal, not only for her
dedicated help with editing the manuscript, putting it
on computer and designing a beautiful
cover for the first edition,
but also for her role as central guardian
angel over this project,
always finding solutions to any kind
of problem that occurred;

my clients, for helping me to learn
from their experiences;

and all others who helped this book grow
from an idea into physical form, including
those who inspired me recently to republish
the manuscript, and those who have supported
me with endorsements for the book.

NOTICE TO THE READER

The ideas and suggestions presented in this book reflect only the personal opinion of the author. They are not meant to replace or compete with professional medical advice, for which the reader needs to consult his or her personal physician, who is qualified to provide correct medical diagnosis and treatment.

TABLE OF CONTENTS

INTRODUCTION

*W*hen a series of articles that were originally written independently over a period of four years are gathered in a book, there are two consequences for the reader. One very nice aspect is that the reader can start reading any chapter of the book, whatever topic interests him or her, because each chapter is able to stand alone. Another perhaps less attractive aspect, but one which is inevitable, is that there is some repetition of certain themes about which the author feels very strongly; the themes of the consequences of a judgmental attitude and that our mind creates the state of health or illness which our body experiences pop up a number of times.

However, the fact that the articles gathered here have generated such a wealth of positive responses through the past few years has encouraged me to present them here, even in this imperfect form. Another important motive has been that I firmly believe that it is vastly important for our entire human family to gain a better understanding of the concepts that are discussed here and learn to express them in their lives.

I have been happy to observe in the two decades that have passed since this book was first published, that many more excellent books have become available, that have helped a much larger audience understand the significance of the mind-body connection in health and illness.

It is my sincere and humble hope that the contemplations presented in the chapters that follow, may also serve as little stepping stones for the reader, to show or remind him or her how we can all work on improving the quality of our lives. As more and more of us get involved with this magnificent process, we will indeed create a new and better world.

CHAPTER 1

ON CAR MAINTENANCE, BODY MAINTENANCE, AND PRIORITIES

Being from Amsterdam, the Netherlands, where everything is so close together you can usually walk, use a bike, or take a tram or bus to get to where you need to go, I noticed a big difference when I came to the United States. Here you cannot expect to get to where you need to go by walking, bicycling, or using public transportation unless you have unlimited time and patience. I found Americans usually have neither the time nor the patience, so they have cars to take them where they need to go, quickly and conveniently.

They are aware that a car needs more than just the right fuel. To function properly, it needs enough engine oil plus a variety of other car body fluids that need to be maintained on a regular basis.. In short, cars need a good care program. Car owners are usually aware of this. They spend time, money, and energy on this program, so they know they can trust their vehicles to serve their needs for a long time.

However, in order to be able to enjoy our nice American cars, we need another vehicle to perform well—our bodies. I realize this does not look like any kind of enlightening statement—yet it reflects the truth.

Although our cars can be expected to last some five to fifteen years and our bodies are meant to last well over one hundred years; we are aware that both kinds of vehicles need proper maintenance, yet we somehow do not get to the body-maintenance part.

Rushed and stressed as we are, not only do we put poor-quality fast food in our fuel tanks, but we also do not seem to find the time to exercise all the body parts enough to keep them in shape. While we spend money for car tune-ups on a regular basis, we feel that for the time being, we cannot spend money for a body tune-up of any kind.

Many kinds of good stress-reduction treatments are available through a variety of bodywork techniques that clear negative energies and restore proper function of the body's energy meridians and ensure all organ systems are energized properly to get the long-lasting performance we need and expect. But although we do not hesitate to spend $80.00 for a power radiator flush, and while we can get a good colonic irrigation for the same amount of money, we will say again that we cannot afford it, denying ourselves a great way to remove accumulated and impacted old toxic waste from our bodies' exhaust pipes. This treatment would definitely assist our body's ability to last longer if included in a regular maintenance program——especially if we do not eat properly all the time.

So what is it that makes us favor the maintenance of our expendable, factory-made cars over that of our sacred, irreplaceable physical vehicles; this special gift of God that we were given to use wisely and reverently? I think I have found the answer. I would like to be wrong, though, for it is not a nice answer. Americans see their cars as a special investment; they are reminded of this every month when they have to come up with the monthly payment. And they know it says in the financing contract that they have to take good care of the vehicle and ensure proper maintenance or the financing agreement could be revoked. And, of course, you do not let what is expensive go to waste. However, we tend not to value very much what comes free, a sad but true aspect of human nature.

So, interestingly, our physical bodies would be better off and get better maintenance if we had to make monthly payments for them. However, many people end up making big monthly payments as a consequence of no preventative maintenance on their bodies when expensive repairs, like a coronary bypass operation or hip replacement, become inevitable. And yet the majority of people don't practice preventative body maintenance. Why isn't this kind of education for people coming from the medical profession? Again, the answer is obvious and not nice. Educating people about how to maintain their bodies in good health would be a threat to a major part of our present medical-care system, which, sadly, has too many elements of an illness industry——because illness means business. So do not count on your doctor here; don't even blame him or her. It's time for us to wake up to the reality that proper maintenance of our bodies is a necessity if we do not want to leave this earthly plane untimely, crippled, and in pain.

So take action. Start putting aside money each month for your body's maintenance just as you do for your car, and know that your body will appreciate it and show you that clearly as your body-maintenance program progresses. There are a great variety of ways to get professional assistance with

1) Proper exercise
2) Learning about better fuel (nutrition)
3) Proper detoxification through colonics or fasting programs
4) Stress-release programs
5) Release of old, restrictive patterns of thinking and feeling
6) Learning to meditate

Allow yourself to feel drawn to one area to start. Do not jump on all six at once. Know that if you properly practice the principles taught through these six systems, your life will expand in a most enjoyable manner, and your body, designed to last many hundreds of years, will definitely not wear out at age seventy or eighty. Instead, it will allow you, in this lifetime, to reach deep into this special twenty-first century, which will be as we are promised, the beginning of a millennium of peace—a totally renewed version of human civilization in proper alignment with the laws of nature and the universe. Be sure to be there! Prepare your body to last! It will be a divine blessing that you will have earned through your efforts. So get with it, and have a good time.

Why don't you write down your plans for *your* new body-maintenance program here? Or—at least—think about them now.

CHAPTER 2

DO WE NEED TO BE VEGETARIANS FOR OUR SPIRITUAL GROWTH?

Life is a wonderful teacher of relativity and balance. If I had had to answer this question forty-eight years ago, when I finished my medical training, I would not have hesitated one moment to say, "Of course not! Why risk becoming deficient in vitamin B12 or other vitamins and minerals and eventually get sick? And what do you mean by *spiritual growth* anyway?"

The brainwashing in medical school suggesting that vegetarianism is a health-threatening practice, inviting vitamin deficiencies and disease, is not to be underestimated in its effect upon the medical advice given by thousands of well-meaning doctors. They were never properly trained in nutrition, so we should not blame them.

Since 1970, I've gradually become more interested in nutrition. I found in my work as an ear, nose, and throat surgeon in Holland that recurring tonsillitis, otitis, and sinusitis were often related to improper nutrition patterns and could be corrected through proper nutrition to treat these symptoms of imbalance instead of surgery.

By reducing the intake of toxic chemicals such as pesticides and preservatives; by eating, whenever possible, organic foods, which also protects us from ingesting GMO foods; and by reducing our sugar intake (currently in the United States sugar is also GMO if not organic); we will significantly reduce the toxicity in our bodies and improve our acid-alkaline balance, thus avoiding the excess acidity that is the inevitable result of relying on fast foods for our nutrition.

Likewise, we stop sugar's assault on the immune system, allowing it to be more effective in fighting off infection, especially if we take some well-chosen vitamin and mineral supplements until health and balance are restored.

If anyone had asked me the same question thirty-five years ago, I would have answered, "Of course we should all be vegetarians! Not only for our spiritual growth but for our good health and longevity. And look at the ethical aspects!"

By that time, I was aware of some statistics about longevity and the incidence of degenerative diseases and cancer, showing clearly that good health and a long-life expectancy are obviously related to balanced protein and low animal-fat diet. The proper diet is preferably 80 percent alkaline foods like fresh vegetables and fruits and only 20 percent acid foods such as proteins (meats, fish, dairy), starches, sugar, alcohol, coffee, and soft drinks—in short, all the elements of American fast-food culture.

If you have doughnuts and coffee for breakfast, a double cheeseburger with a Pepsi for lunch, and spaghetti with meat sauce and a salad followed by ice cream for dinner, then the dinner salad has to balance the 98-percent-acid foods––which is obviously impossible. This nutrition pattern has not given Americans the lead in world longevity statistics; by now they are about number seventeen on the list, whereas in those parts of Asia where rice, fish, and vegetables are still the main foods, we find many more centenarians and less untimely death by degenerative diseases. The Essenes, a spiritual community who lived near the Dead Sea in Israel during the days of Jesus, were strict vegetarians who ate most of their vegetables uncooked, lived in total harmony with nature, and reportedly reached an average age of 120 years. They left us a beautiful spiritual heritage as recorded in *The Gospel of the Essenes* and other books by Edmund Bordeaux Szekely, which were, in part, translated from the Dead Sea Scrolls. They demonstrated clearly how the Essenes' healthy diet, life style, and longevity were linked to their spiritual philosophy. We are what we eat and what we think in our hearts.

Eating a healthy, balanced diet that pays attention to the freshness of food and to the necessary acid-alkaline balance leaves little space for big servings of carbohydrates and animal proteins like meat. Giving priority to regular exercise in fresh air to assist in our elimination of toxins, is both conducive to a clear, relaxed state of mind (which will be better able to attune itself to our higher nature in meditation) and to a healthy body, which will serve us faithfully for many years.

Again, let us now ask ourselves the question, "Do we all need to be vegetarians for our spiritual growth?" My answer has to be "well, maybe or probably"; it cannot be just a "yes," for there are some aspects at which we still need to look. Although we are all unique individuals, we fit into certain constitutional body types. In the Orient, we find dominant Yin or Yang types. The Yin-type person is long, slender, not too well-grounded, more inclined to daydream or meditate than to do body-building; they are creative, but find it difficult to pursue their manifestation in this physical dimension; they are not too interested in eating and will eat as lightly as possible, preferably vegetarian. The pituitary body type, in the Abravanel body-type system, also fits this description, as does the leptosome type in the old European Kretschmer typology tradition. Astrologically, certain water and air signs like Pisces and sometimes Aquarius resonate more or less with this description. In contrast, the Yang body type is sturdier or even chubby, with more earthy inclinations, enjoys exercise, is very energetic, can do with little sleep, enjoys the heavier salty foods like meat and potatoes, and finds it more difficult to calm down as would be needed for meditation. The adrenal body type in the Abravanel system, and the pyknic type according to Kretschmer, with earth and fire elements best represented by Taurus and sometimes Aries, are to a certain extent all similar in this sense.

Why do we need to look at all this here? It is obvious that all "earthy" body-types of the Yang group will reach a better balance if they are able to rise above their inclination to density in their diet and life-style. A vegetarian diet would be quite helpful to most of them, maybe not all as there is also an influence of our blood type on our body's dietary preference, e.g., a blood type A generally thrives more on a strictly vegetarian diet than a type O. In contrast with the Yang body types, the less grounded Yin types may tend to drift off the planet without the grounding effect that animal-derived foods like dairy products, eggs, fish, poultry or occasionally some red meat like lamb will provide. For them, it can definitely be helpful to arrive at a proper physical and mental balance by partaking of these foods as needed. I can speak from experience here. Being a classical Yin, pituitary type, leptosome Pisces with blood type O myself, it has proven to be impossible for me to stay in proper balance on a strict vegetarian diet without animal products. I tried it for several years and found it to be wonderful for meditating, but not for functioning properly in a busy medical practice, where a lot of well-grounded physical energy was needed.

In conclusion, maybe it is not yet necessary for all of us to become vegetarians right now in order to grow spiritually. Nonetheless, we need to practice much more nutritional awareness than we do at this time. Lack of understanding of the importance of the acid-alkaline balance we need to provide at the dinner table has had serious effects on our life expectancy. In addition, thoughtless use of drugs to stop the body's alarm signals such as headaches, frequent colds or rheumatic pains, indicating that the acidity level is far too high, has made this even worse.

To nourish our spiritual nature, we need food which still contains the subtle life force energy. We can only get this energy from unadulterated fresh foods, whether it be from vegetables, fruits, fish or meat. Freezing any of these will destroy most of the subtle energy and nourishment they would have provided; cooking all our vegetables means losing most of the subtle life force as well. A great way to add alkalinity and subtle energy to our food is to use sprouts, e.g. mung beans and lentil sprouts in our salads. Soaking the beans and lentils for a few hours in a glass jar for the first day, and rinsing them 3 times a day on the 2nd and 3rd days, will produce tasty and very nutritious sprouts, which can thereafter be stored in the refrigerator. Sunflower seeds, sprouted in this manner are also a great source of energy.

Let us use our spiritual and physical body awareness to nourish ourselves properly. When we go out to buy our food let us try to sense in the store which foods attract our attention that day; they may well be what our body needs most. If we buy those foods and go home and prepare them fresh, using part of the vegetables raw in a salad, we will feel more energized after our meals instead of tired and sleepy.

With diligent attention to what we eat we will definitely enhance the spiritual quality of our life, whether or not we need a little meat to stay grounded. And if we do, let us be aware and appreciative of the sacrifice that the animal kingdom is willing to make for us, as its collective consciousness realizes that as we evolve, they will as well. Remember this when saying grace over your meal, which, by the way, also quite effectively increases the subtle energy in it. Bon appetit.

What diet changes can <u>you</u> make to rejuvenate your body?

CHAPTER 3

IS REJUVENATION
REALLY POSSIBLE?

Throughout man's history, the aging process of the physical body has never been very appealing and countless attempts have been made to break out of this pattern and maintain, if not regain, a youthful state. Millions of elixirs of youth have been ingested or applied externally, and many people have learned the painful and often expensive lesson that the secret of eternal youth cannot yet be ingested or rubbed on.

If it is true what we find in several spiritual teachings that the human body was designed to last more than two thousand years, then there are obviously quite a number of things that have gone wrong since our first human "test models" lived on this planet in the early Lemurian days.

We are by now quite aware of the fact that we do not live in the Garden of Eden anymore. But even though Adam and Eve were dismissed from there, they were reported to have lived about 900 years, and so did the first

10 generations that followed. From Noah's son, Shem, until Abraham, the next 10 generations of our Biblical forefathers lived an average life span of 312 years, as computed by Gabriel Cousens, M.D. in his excellent book "Spiritual Nutrition and the Rainbow Diet." He attributes the drastic reduction of our life span since Noah's time to the introduction of meat into the human diet. Since then, we have managed to reduce our life expectancy even more to about 75 years; less than 20% of Abraham's, and not even 4% of our early Lemurian life span.

This seems totally tragic. However, there is a positive aspect to it. If we realize that we are timeless, ageless, immortal, spiritual light beings who inhabit an earth body to enjoy the opportunity for intense spiritual growth that the earth plane provides, then this extreme life span reduction has allowed us some 27 more new, fresh opportunities to start again after we messed up, without being burdened by the memory of having messed up our life. This is just one aspect of the way we have totally polluted our planet and also polluted, weakened and even degenerated our physical body. Looking back at what we have done, it appears to be quite a bizarre way to evolve and grow spiritually.

However, not all hope is lost. We have by now arrived at the point where the average world citizen has become aware of the great need to collectively clean up our act and our planet as a top priority to survive. I feel quite encouraged by this observation, and would like to add that, as we do this clean-up job, our potential for longevity and rejuvenation will start to increase again.

We can gradually begin to attack the causes of aging we know by making the following changes:

1) Shift to organic ways of growing our food, eliminating GMO foods, pesticides and all other forms of chemical pollution and irradiation.

2) Shift to eating as many unprocessed foods as possible, to maximize our ability to take in the subtle life force in our food.

3) Shift away from excessive use of stimulants like coffee, sugar, alcohol, nicotine and drugs. This may be quite difficult for many, who at this time still consider these elements as their primary nutrition, and which quite effectively accelerate their aging process.

4) Develop and stay with a personal exercise program, understanding our body's need to exercise, in order to effectively burn up waste materials, keep our cardiovascular and neuromuscular systems in shape, and release tension and stress.

5) Learn to avoid overexposure to certain kinds of electrical, magnetic and light energy. This occurs in many ways, e.g. overexposure to TV, computer screens and keyboards, wifi fields, microwave energy, etc. All these will drain our energy, and make us feel fatigued, weak and stressed. Negative earth currents cause geopathic stress, a tremendously underestimated contributing factor in ill health. And, of course, overexposure

to sunlight causes premature skin aging and can promote skin cancer.

6) Give higher priority to the elimination of our stress, and, if that is not possible, engage in activities that will help to release it. Most people have no idea how severely their health and life expectancy are threatened by the stress with which they live. Stress puts our body in the high adrenalin fight-or-flight mode, which is incompatible with effective digestive function as well as with our ability to sleep soundly ; the incomplete digestion can also create toxic metabolites even out of healthy foods.

If this condition persists, it will bring about premature cellular aging and a shortened life span.

There are many ways to overcome stress without outside help, which can be done according to personal preference, either through the many kinds of physical recreational activities or through meditation, as mentioned in our next category.

7) Build a better awareness of and control over our predominant thought patterns. The human mind has unlimited potential for growth and expansion which can be developed through proper attunement and meditation. However, it can also set itself to create limiting, stressful, worrying, judgmental, unloving and fearful thought patterns; and we do not realize that this mental rigidity and constriction has been largely

responsible for many psychosomatic diseases, as well as premature aging and death.

In many of the teachings that were given through Edgar Cayce, the statement can be found that "Spirit is the life, mind is the builder, and the physical is the result." If we have ever been aware of this truth before, we now seem to have lost that awareness; otherwise we would never have allowed our minds to build not only the psychosomatic disease patterns, but also those that have led to the many other degenerative diseases with which we now struggle. Instead, we would be like the master souls, living in a radiant, healthy body that would keep us looking like 25 year olds for many hundreds of years.

Are we to conclude then that we can only rejuvenate ourselves by "what we eat and what we think" or by our own actions? Definitely not. There are various ways in which we can greatly benefit from the release of stress, and the cleansing, strengthening, relaxing and realigning of our physical, etheric, emotional and mental vehicles. Our own intuition is usually the best guidance of where we should start … with massage or reflexology treatments, colonic irrigation, counseling, spiritual healing or some other method.

It is essential that we find a therapist with whom we feel safe enough to allow ourselves to release all of those inadequate protections that we have built around us in the past, and to open ourselves up again to the whisperings of the divine spark within us. As we learn to intensify that communication, we will feel how the stressful and otherwise limiting and negative aspects of life gradually lose their grip on us. By becoming younger and more joyful at heart again, we will exude this in our improved health and in our outward appearance, literally through our skin. For then our soul can demonstrate that it still remembers from the early Lemurian days that continuous rejuvenation is still really possible, as it has always been.

You can now expand your personal rejuvenation program that you planned on page 12!

CHAPTER 4

ILLNESS AS A NUISANCE AND OPPORTUNITY

Metaphysically interested people usually know or are at least familiar with the idea that nothing happens in this world without meaning or cause. When we see people who are workaholics or overindulgent in other ways (like consuming way too much ice cream in a short time), it is not too difficult to understand why they get sick when they do. We can see that too much work without relaxation (playing) time depletes their energy and, at the physical level, their immune system. This opens the door to illness that will force them to lay in bed, rest, recover and rebalance their energy. Likewise, the ice cream "over-consumer" may experience an intense physical cleansing action like diarrhea which will at least discourage them from replenishing the supply of their favorite brand for a while.

Somehow, when illness strikes in our own house, it appears to be more difficult to retain our metaphysical understanding that we are so quick to apply to others. Let me give you an example. A young, promising psychic and healer gives a lecture on "How to Develop Our Inner Vision Faster" in the back room of a metaphysical bookstore. This topic draws 50 people into the small space available. One of them has a cold and sneezes repeatedly, even through the closing meditation. This means that enough of the fine mist of common cold virus particles are delivered into the room for all attending to partake of. However, not everyone attending will "catch" this cold; only a few will––only those whose bodies were waiting for this opportunity to eliminate certain undesirable energy patterns.

If you were one of those few, you might very well find yourself responding by blaming both the sneezer at the lecture and the virus itself. You would not realize that they were both needed vehicles to present you with an opportunity to either eliminate the overacidity in your body or maybe release feelings of anger or strong irritation toward the people you live with and love most. We often hold these negative energy patterns in our paranasal sinuses. Our body is actually quite happy to have this nice chance to eliminate the excess acidity, negative emotions, or both, wrapped in our nasal secretions, while we, unaware of either one, are annoyed with this same process.

Of course, this mechanism is not limited to colds; it holds true for the entire spectrum of human illnesses that we find ourselves facing at this time. Some of these appear to be so complex, like chronic fatigue syndrome, that in searching for the exact role of the Epstein-Barr virus in this disorder, we lose sight of the fact that we attract this condition by paralyzing our immune system with a lack of enthusiasm for life, being bored, not enjoying our work, or in short, being caught up in a negative network of thoughts and feelings. This makes it impossible for our body to function properly when it is deprived of the energizing effects of self-love and appreciation, joyfulness and fulfillment. Insight into these mechanisms is essential for the cure of all illnesses that are believed to be the scourge of mankind at this time. In "regular" A.M.A.-approved medical research centers, enormous amounts of money and energy are spent every day in desperate attempts to find physical agents, like drugs, to cure cancer, AIDS and cardiovascular disease, all three of which are already being cured holistically by overcoming the mental, emotional and nutritional imbalances that are the building blocks of all of them.

In actuality, there is not a single illness that truly originates at the physical level. Instead, all illnesses originate in the subtle realms at the mental and emotional level. Therefore it must also be possible to cure them there. This means that once we are armed with this insight and apply it, there can no longer be incurable diseases.

I have been counseling a lady who was diagnosed with malignant melanoma, a form of cancer, which in her case had spread throughout her body. The conventional A.M.A. medical approach to this is still as it was 50 years ago, focused only on surgical interventions, and/or radiation and chemotherapy. And while this approach may still be inevitable in some cases, this wonderful lady was able to gather the self-knowledge and insight to help her better monitor her thought and emotional patterns, and "catch" and eradicate her negative patterns of self-judgment, unworthiness, inadequacy and being bored with a life that appeared to have little meaning ; all of these, as she could then see, became the energetic cause of this illness. It was very difficult for her at first to replace her negative emotions with positive ones—like building more faith, utilizing prayer and affirmations in order to attain a more joyful state of mind and be grateful for this opportunity to overcome this enormous challenge ; but it was great to witness her excitement when her condition started to improve against all medical expectations.

In conclusion, whether an illness we "get" is minor or catastrophic, it can be cured if we are willing and able to take up the challenge, and change whatever is necessary to rebalance ourselves. While we work through our "nuisance", let us be grateful indeed for the opportunity, given in a clear and precise message, pointing out the imbalances we need to correct, which allows us to live our lives full of happiness and fulfillment as was divinely planned.

Make some notes here on your ideas and insights on what <u>you</u> can learn from your physical weakness or illness.

CHAPTER 5

PAST LIFE REGRESSION:
WHAT'S THE POINT?

Recent statistics indicate one out of three Americans believes in reincarnation. Some 50 years ago, perhaps 4 out of 100 Americans would have answered positive.

This striking increase in our awareness of the larger pattern governing our earthly experience cannot be accidental. Along with our human family's growing awareness and understanding of the phenomenon of the near death experience, we are learning that we are not just these bodies that we inhabit, but we are spiritual beings that use the earth plane through a long series of incarnations to learn and grow.

While the cosmic energies that are being sent to our planet at this time are very conducive to expanding this awareness of ourselves as spiritual beings, many old, very evolved souls are now coming in with a greater capacity to remember their past lives and give accurate, verifiable information about their last earthly life experience, complete with names, addresses and all. This is documented in many books about reincarnation, spiritual rebirth, transformation into the awareness of the continuity of life, and so on. So there is a snowball effect. The ones who remember their past lives are helping others to start considering the possibility that this might indeed be true. And through an experience, such as a psychic reading, a rebirthing or past life regression, they can confirm that this feels indeed like their truth too.

This is how it happened for me. When I had my first psychic reading I had just begun to consider that I might indeed have lived before. I was quite amazed to learn about a certain character trait I had had while being a temple architect in Egypt –– the inability to delegate work for fear that mistakes would be made. I find myself some 4000 years and around 50 lifetimes later, still struggling with this problem. How slow we can be to learn! So then I was definitely convinced that the lady, who did not know me when she did the reading by mail, could not have made this up, nor a number of other traits she mentioned I had in past lives, that I can recognize in myself even today.

This reveals something important about past life awareness. We do not start to believe in reincarnation just because somebody else tells us that they do. We need our own personal experience, and when we can acknowledge that as our truth, then we know it for sure from then on. Once we have this awareness of our past lives, we develop a natural curiosity about who we were and what we did. The fact that many beginners in this field have developed a strong conviction that they once were Napoleon, Paracelsus, Joan of Arc, Cleopatra or Nefertiti has brought some discredit to the concept of reincarnation. A possible explanation for this phenomenon might be that many of us have had a lifetime experience with these leaders and have strong memories in our memory banks about them, which we then misinterpret only in part.

While it is obviously beneficial to recognize the grander pattern of life in our reincarnation cycles, many people feel that it is meaningless to delve into the past because we have to live now and make the best of this lifetime. While the latter part of this statement is true, we will miss special opportunities for spiritual growth and the release of mental and emotional limitations if we are not willing to look at our past.

While we may now be wonderful, sweet people who would not harm a fly, we can safely assume that we have not always been this way. In our soul urge to learn through experience, we have done just about everything that people can do to each other, and as the cosmic laws require, when we inflict an act of violence upon another person, we will have to learn what it is like to undergo that same experience. Thus we have all killed and been killed, raped and been raped, tortured and been tortured; we have not just been healers and been healed.

It requires courage and a non-judgmental attitude to accept a past life regression, to open our personal Pandora's box and discover the interactions we have had in the past with, most likely, the same people that are emotionally important in our life now. Many of us are still struggling with the severe emotional impact of events that have happened in past lives. If we are unwilling to look back, we will miss an important opportunity for healing that comes when we review past lives and then heal the memory –– yes, this is distinctly possible.

Many of the fears with which we struggle, like fears of heights, water (which is really a fear of drowning), snakes and spiders, and so on relate to actual memories of violent endings of past lifetimes, which we have not yet been able to heal or release. And as many of our past life actions were not always helpful and hopeful to others, we may have generated strong feelings of guilt, involving a subconscious need for punishment. We may be expressing this need right now through repeated physical injuries, lack of financial success in life, an inability to engage in a positive, supportive relationship, or in a chronic illness, the location of which in the body will be related to where the mental and emotional energy of the guilt is focused. The following are some examples.

A lady came to me with chronic pain and infection in her upper right jaw. Neither her doctor nor her dentist could help her adequately. She had a sense that this had something to do with a past life experience. In the past life regression, she first sees herself as a soldier, dying in battle from wounds to the right jaw and eye. Next, she remembers herself as a beggar in the streets, crippled with very painful sores and ulcers in her upper right jaw.

When specifically suggested to go back to that lifetime where the root cause of these experiences could be found, she saw herself as a young mother, hiding outside under a bridge with a baby in her arms. The baby was crying. As the sound would expose them, she put her hand over the baby's mouth to muffle the sound. When she felt safe to come out, she realized that the baby had died from suffocation.

In reliving the agony of such a moment, we go through a process releasing the pain; and when I asked where in her body she felt the emotional residue of her guilt, she did not speak but just moved her hand to her jaw. I was amazed to realize how this guilt, focused there, had affected her for two lifetimes in the past and again now.

Another example: a talented businessman with great spiritual awareness finds himself unable to maintain a level of financial success. After having done well for a period of time, he would lose everything again. In a past life regression, he remembered a life with very wealthy, but unfeeling, cold-hearted parents. In an effort to disengage himself from them completely, he entered a monastery and took a vow of poverty. As that lifetime was early in the 20th century, it must have been his most recent past life, and that vow of poverty was obviously still affecting him. Revoking that vow of poverty proved to be quite helpful.

Summarizing, we should not delve into our past lives with a focus of curiosity or a search for glamour. But great healing can occur if we undergo past life regressions with a focus of trying to find what emotional residues of past disasters we need to clear that are interfering with our capacity to be successful, happy and healthy in this life. I trust that in the near future the medical profession will become more aware of these powerful causative factors of illness. But for the time being, I would advise anyone struggling with chronic illness, not to wait until their doctor tells them to, but to explore on their own how they can release past life burdens that express themselves in their illness.

So what is the point of past life regression? The point of past life regression is that by accessing and healing our past life burdens, we can then program our mind to rebuild our health, happiness and joy of living, resonating naturally without inhibitions of any kind with the infinite love of our Creator.

Room for any clues <u>you</u> have had that you could have lived before.

CHAPTER 6

ALLOPATHIC OR HOLISTIC
MEDICINE --WHEN DO
WE NEED WHICH?

When we learn in our spiritual studies that we are so much more than just the body we inhabit and that we build our physical reality with our mind, our attitude toward medicine will change dramatically. Before, we were happy to go to our allopathic physician when we had any physical problem. He would tell us which part or parts would be malfunctioning (like the tonsils in the case of a recurrent tonsillitis) and he would tell us that we would be better off to have them removed as they were "rotten." So we would happily undergo a tonsillectomy, expecting that the surgery would cure us.

As we develop a stronger inclination toward holistic philosophy, we begin to understand that all body functions and parts are designed to work in perfect balance and we start to reject the idea that a tonsillectomy is the solution for recurrent tonsillitis. We start looking for answers to the question: what in the body is out of balance and is causing this problem? We start listening to advice––that we need to change our diet (to reduce the toxicity in the body) and, on the emotional level, we start searching for ways to express our creativity better, rather than stifling it––which is, by the way, an important aspect in recurrent tonsillitis in children. In other words, as we expand in spiritual understanding and awareness, we will move away from traditional medicine and follow a more holistic medical philosophy. The family physician we choose will reflect that.

Can we turn away from traditional, allopathic, drugs-and-surgery medicine entirely? Somehow we all know that would not be wise. If we break a leg, we do not go to our holistic physician for repair. We know that the traditional immobilization of the fracture or, in the case of severe dislocation, even surgical repair is the way to go. Sometimes, however, people develop such faith in the holistic approach that they will not seek help in the traditional medical circuit, even when they really need it. Such was the case of a man with a severely enlarged prostate gland. He was almost unable to urinate, and had begun to develop an ascending type of urinary tract infection. He consulted a holistic physician and became very angry when he was told he should see a urologist immediately. He said, "I did not come here to have you tell me that! I want you to help me!"

So we can see here that with acute mechanical problems, allopathic medicine has superior answers. However, allopathic medicine does not have the best answers for chronic degenerative disorders because it is unwilling to look at the greater dynamic patterns that cause these disorders to manifest. It is wonderful that it is now possible to replace a hip joint. It is not wonderful that many people with arthritic hip pains are just given painkillers and cortisone, until the hip joint is so severely deteriorated that hip replacement surgery seems to be the only solution. There are a whole range of holistic approaches that could have stopped the hip problem from progressing or might even have cured it. Holistic medicine, by using nutritional counseling, mineral and vitamin supplementation, physiotherapy, massage, exercise programs, possibly acupuncture or even intuitive counseling –– to find out what emotional energy is locked up in that hip joint –– has the better answers. So we can see that allopathic medicine's limited concept of the human body considerably limits its answers to chronic disease.

Cancer is a special and dramatic category of chronic disease. It is a big challenge for any holistically inclined patient, who is diagnosed with it, to face the dilemma and decide which way to go. This will be addressed further in the chapter on cancer therapy.

Summarizing, we have looked at some general guidelines about when to turn to which form of medicine, but of course, there are no real rules to follow. The best guidance will always be that which is received in a meditative state, through our connection with the divine, where all answers are known. Let everyone of us, who may suddenly at any moment in time be faced with the need to seek medical help, use these reflections to refrain from being overly judgmental or resentful toward allopathic medicine, as it may be necessary for us to turn there for help in our hour of need. But, let us at the same time be in charge of what we allow to be done to our body, always seeking the answer that will give our body the best chance to rebalance, to strengthen, and to purify, so we will be better able to resonate with and amplify divine love and light —— as that is what we are all here to do.

Plan here, where you can seek help for <u>your</u> specific physical challenges.

CHAPTER 7

CAN WE OVERCOME
OUR ALLERGIES?

In this chapter, I will not go extensively into the contemporary medical and nutritionists' ideas about diagnosis and treatment of allergies —– I do not feel that there exists a need for that here, as just about everyone has already been exposed to these ideas in one way or another. In addition, I do not exactly agree with them, for they tend to give the allergy, when diagnosed, the weight of scientific confirmation, and with a sense of finality, program this into the mind of the patient. Worst of all, they claim that now the real cause of the problem has been found and can be treated.

In the case of food allergies, where elimination of the supposed offenders is the main therapeutic approach, many people suffer greatly from a lifetime sentence of eliminating so many important foods from their diet that mealtimes turn into times of discipline rather than enjoyment. People can become really very depressed about these restrictions, which at the subconscious level, are experienced as an undeserved punishment.

The strange thing about this is, that even among spiritually aware doctors and nutritionists, this traditional approach is usually still maintained. It is as if there is a blind spot in their awareness of the fact, which was formulated so well by Edgar Cayce almost 100 years ago: "Spirit is the life, mind is the builder and the physical is the result." This clearly indicates that there is no condition at all that truly originates at the physical level, and that there is no physical condition or illness that cannot be healed through the mind.

And even before Cayce, at the beginning of the 20th century, Rudolf Steiner, who founded the anthroposophical medical philosophy in Germany, had stated that there are patterns of thought and feeling that will make the body susceptible to allergies. He said that we have to come into this earth plane and this earth body with enthusiasm, and a certain degree of fighting spirit, which we need to win the battle with the food we eat. We need to be able to draw the nourishment out of our food without being affected by its waste which we must eliminate. If we are heavily burdened, either by past life memories as we come in or by present life difficulties, we may feel weakened in our capacity to deal with this aspect of life properly, and may experience this world as an unsafe or even hostile environment. We are now beginning to realize that the real cause of a low thyroid function is also a lack of enthusiasm for life, as is explained further in the next chapter.

There are some recent medical insights about allergies that can help us to gain a better understanding of the actual mechanisms at work here. We know that when we think, the electrical activity in our brain cells produces and releases a whole range of chemical messengers which allow the brain cells to "talk" to each other and to all other cells in the body as well. However, what has now been found is that the circulating white blood cells of our immune system are also capable of producing each and every one of these chemical messengers that the brain cells produce when we think. It appears therefore correct to assume that these immune cells can also think, make decisions, act and interact. E.g. a circulating immune cell can recognize, attack, encapsulate and kill a virus particle, like a warrior, effectively eliminating the enemy. So then, an allergy is really a challenging consequence of our immune system's capacity to listen to and act on certain signals that come from our own mind.

When these signals (in the form of allergic reactions or symptoms) indicate that this world is an unsafe or even hostile environment, this will most likely originate from our subconscious mind when it has been fed by our thoughts and feelings of frustration, aggression experienced from other people and, most importantly, a lack of nurturing and joyful experiences.

So we can feel this way even without being aware of it. However, our immune system gets the message and comes to our aid, ready to fight back. This process can eventually reach the point where our immune cells start attacking just about every kind of molecule that comes in from the environment, which is what happens in environmental illness. Or, if we really do not feel good at all about having to function in an earth body, our immune cells may even turn against the tissues of our own body, which is what happens in auto-immune diseases.

Realizing this, it is now clear that dealing therapeutically with allergies only on the physical body level is rather primitive, and can never be totally effective for we are then fighting symptoms or results of the allergic response. Instead we have to move up to the realm of causes, and address the mental and emotional, or even spiritual attitudes that gave the immune system ––via the brain–– the erratic messages. Is it possible to do this effectively, or in other words, can we really overcome our allergies? Most definitely yes! The only condition is that we have to be willing to be introspective, to seek help if needed, to work on changing our experiences in this earth plane, and to heal the memories of struggle and difficulty that we somehow got stuck with.

So here are seven practical steps toward overcoming your allergies:

1) Stop believing that you will have your allergy for the rest of your life even if your allergist or nutritionist told you so. What you believe becomes your truth in the physical plane as you have already found out. You know better now and have already started to change the messages you send your immune system.

2) Do not overextend yourself. In cases of extreme fatigue or exhaustion, allergic reactions tend to get more intense as is illustrated by the severe allergies that are often part of the chronic fatigue syndrome. Give yourself a break, do not let that happen to you.

3) Learn to meditate and practice it every day as a centering exercise and stress release and rejuvenation program - see the last two chapters on meditation.

4) Affirm that this world is a safe and friendly place to be in and be aware of your worthiness to receive success, prosperity and love.

5) Work at releasing guilt and self-judgements. This may require spiritual counseling or healing, which will give you the additional benefit of assistance with recognizing and healing those subconscious patterns of thought and feeling that have led to the allergic response of your immune system. These may go back to before this lifetime! For example: a man, who was very allergic to cats, was reminded through spiritual guidance that he was still working through the fearful subconscious memory of having been killed by a tiger in a past life!

6) Treat your body with more love and appreciation. It has been the battlefield of expression of your misperceptions of life in this earth plane, and you have not appreciated it, or, even worse, you have resented it. Make up for that right now! Tell your body and tell your immune system that you

love them and that you want them to be relaxed and happy –– there really is no war to be fought! Treat yourself to a good massage or any other body work treatment to help release stress and which approaches the body in a loving and caring manner.

7) Improve your diet and life style where you can. Make sure that you take the time to sit down and eat meals that you enjoy and which are nourishing to your subtle vehicles as well as your physical body. That is why you need your fresh fruits and vegetables. Be careful with sugar, coffee and alcohol. Give up smoking. Find an exercise program that suits your body's needs and that will help it to feel more appreciated and cared for.

If this program appears to be too difficult for you, do not worry. You can always go back to or even stay with your allergist who will be happy to give you drugs, shots and a long list of taboo foods and activities for the rest of your life. But why would you not give this program a fair chance to overcome your allergy? After all, what is really required of you is just a willingness to eliminate some illusions about your life on earth that you have held in your mind, and start expressing more love toward yourself and toward your physical environment. In your new understanding, this environment will be a truly beautiful expression of the limitless love and the joyful creativity of its Maker.

Room to plan <u>your</u> personal allergy-overcoming program.

CHAPTER 8

LOW THYROID AND
DEPRESSION -- WHICH
CAME FIRST?

Imagine this scenario, which happens countless times in doctors' offices all over the world of Western medicine: Melanie, a woman in her mid-forties complains to her family physician about lack of energy and a sense of depression; it seems harder than ever to get through the day's work. The doctor conducts a physical exam where nothing is found and orders a few blood tests. In a few days, Melanie hears from him over the telephone. The cause of her problem has been found. She has a low thyroid function which has caused her lack of energy and her depression, and if she just takes her thyroid medication for the rest of her life, she will be fine.

Is this the whole truth and nothing but the truth? Since Melanie has been working on expanding her spiritual awareness and understanding for many years, she was not quite sure about this and asked me for a second opinion. I had to agree with her intuitive sense that she had not been told the whole truth; not because her physician had withheld information from her but rather because his belief system did not acknowledge the fact that no organ or endocrine gland in the human body will ever start malfunctioning spontaneously without there being a cause for that malfunction in the mental or emotional realms. Our mind is always creating either balance –– good health –– or imbalance –– resulting in illness.

In the case of the thyroid gland, let us look at some interactions here. The thyroid gland, shaped like a butterfly and draped over the lower anterior side of our larynx, is like the carburetor of our metabolic engine. It needs to be well tuned to our body's metabolic needs. If set too high it will burn up our metabolic energy resources, causing a sensation of being hot, nervous tremors, diarrhea and weight loss. If set too low, it will create a sluggish metabolism, constipation, weight gain, a sensation of being cold, a lack of energy, and often a feeling of depression –– "I cannot do it." Thyroid activity is regulated by the pituitary gland, located at the base of the brain. It measures thyroid hormone levels in the blood and sends out a thyroid stimulating hormone if thyroid activity is too low. The pituitary gland also responds to biochemical messages from our brain, i.e. the thoughts we create in our mind. While there are some rare causes of thyroid insufficiency related to mineral deficiencies such as iodine-deficiency or to pituitary gland failure, the great majority of cases of low thyroid activity is a response to mental influences.

We know specifically that if we find earthly life increasingly difficult and lose our spiritual motivation or enthusiasm to be here in the earth plane, this is translated into biochemical messages that will result in the partial shutting down of our physical engine's carburetor. So now we can see that it is only a partial truth that taking thyroid hormone medication will cure the depression. It can jump start the metabolic engine and help with the secondary depression due to the lack of physical energy. But the primary or spiritual depression will remain unaddressed or masked.

Taking thyroid hormone medication has an additional disadvantage which is comparable to putting on reading glasses when the lenses of our eyes begin to become less flexible. By taking the medication the body senses the gland's product is already there and it decides there is no need to work anymore! This will generate a need for more medication, just as our eye lenses, when we "help" them with the reading glasses, will also lose their motivation to work and cause us to need even stronger reading glasses.

So obviously we should not settle for anything less than the whole truth about everything as we strive to keep ourselves healthy in body, mind and spirit. Let us be brave enough to face the probability of a reduced enthusiasm for earthly life if our thyroid function is low. And let us search for ways to heal that primary, subtle depression. This may require help in the realm of healing, counseling, and learning of meditation techniques which will help to resolve conflicts that we hold in our subconscious mind.

Remember that our body does not respond exclusively to biochemical messages from our conscious mind. It responds just as much, if not more so, to the great storehouse of emotional turmoil, that our subconscious mind has become through its memories of many lifetimes of difficult experiences without adequate avenues for release.

So, summarizing, let us go for the true healing process rather than accepting the quick fixes of our thyroid pills or reading glasses, which will only invite further deterioration. Let us work at healing our inner wounds and raising ourselves up by appreciating the beauty and special gifts and opportunities that life on earth offers us.

Imagine how wonderful you will feel at the end of your life knowing you managed to successfully work through all of your life's lessons, including your thyroid lesson, rather than miss out by accepting the thyroid pills as the solution to your problem. So, always check your intuition before your believe your doctor!

This does not mean that all patients with a low thyroid should totally refuse to take any thyroid medication. I suggest that they accept the pills as a necessary help for their body in the beginning, but they should not delay in working to eliminate the need for them.

How about starting an eye exercise program? Or working in other ways to replace <u>your</u> quick fixes with real problem solving?

CHAPTER 9

A CASE OF EPILEPSY

E pilepsy, especially the form that expresses itself in "grand mal" seizures, has always been an impressive form of disease. The Romans called it "Morbus Sacer," meaning sacred illness, suggesting that the gods were somehow involved in it. In the Middle Ages, an epileptic was considered possessed by demons.

Contemporary medicine recognizes a number of possible causes for it: a stroke, intoxication, head trauma and metabolic disorders. However, 97% of patients have idiopathic epilepsy, meaning that no cause can be found and the only comfort offered to them is limited to an anti-epileptic medication, which must be taken as long as they live. How can we expand on this sad and limited view here and apply our spiritual understanding that all physical disease starts out as a mental and emotional imbalance, which needs to be addressed and healed at these levels?

As we study our subtle body anatomy and physiology, we find that the brain just like the eyes, ears and nose is governed and nourished by the energy from the sixth chakra, centrally located on the forehead –– the third eye. This chakra has, since ancient times, been recognized as a doorway to higher wisdom, higher awareness and inner vision. To develop these qualities in our life, we have to be willing to be introspective and try to rise above thoughts and feelings of self-pity when things are difficult, and transcend our thoughts and feelings to where we can see the meaning and purpose of circumstances presented to us as our life's lessons. If we do not develop these qualities, we are likely to remain caught in a circuit of negative perceptions –– with an abundance of judgments against ourselves and others, such as fear, anger and self-pity. If we hold on to these thought and feeling patterns with enough intensity over a period of time, we may block the energy of this chakra sufficiently to cause a brain disorder of some kind. Specifically, the fear of introspection, or the fear of developing one's intuitive capacities, may ultimately be expressed in this manner.

For example: Jodi, a sweet lady in her early thirties with obvious healing qualities came to me to present her problem. She felt drawn to quit her administrative job in order to pursue her Reiki training to become a healer. However, she felt held back by the fact that she has epilepsy and needs to take her anti-epileptic medication to prevent seizures; she has a strong sense that she should first find a way to heal her epilepsy before she can fully engage in her healing career.

I had to agree with her. So, in our first session we worked on her feelings of guilt, self-judgment and inadequacy about having epilepsy, reestablishing her sense of worthiness to be a healer, and helping her to see herself working through this illness as a specific challenge in her training. We felt that a past life regression would be helpful to understand the true causative levels of fear and judgment that were interfering with proper third-eye chakra functioning. We did this in a second session. Without any difficulty or delay, Jodi first saw a big swastika and then herself as a male German scientist of some kind, in Nazi Germany in the late nineteen thirties, who allowed himself to be pulled into the vortex of all the excitement and the promises for a better future that were offered by Adolf Hitler. As the Nazi leadership was also an occult organization, she had memories of learning to develop psychic powers, but only in the black magic sense of learning to manipulate and control others. By the time this man realized he had been lured into participation in downright evil actions, it was too late to correct it. He was killed in World War II shortly before it was over. Our Jodi came out of that lifetime with an enormous sense of guilt plus an intense fear of opening up psychically again, for subconsciously she associated that with engaging in evil actions. She could understand clearly at that moment how these intense emotions have set the stage for her to have to deal with epilepsy in this lifetime. However, the insights she received in the regression greatly improved her chances to overcome this epilepsy completely.

So, once again, the illnesses that we view as just a burden, or a punishment from God, on the contrary, always bring a fascinating message that we need to be willing to hear and act upon. Sometimes we may require help in having the message clarified for us.

So, if we believe that something can be done, as Jodi did, and if we are willing to act on that belief, then there are no limits to the healing that can be accomplished. Never learn to live with your disease! And do not believe your doctor when he says you must! Start now to take action toward a healthier and happier life.

Which fear and judgment based limiting belief systems can <u>you</u> think of that you have, on which you could start working now?

CHAPTER 10

THE LESSON OF SHINGLES: PEACE OR PAIN

Most of us know that shingles, or herpes zoster as it is officially named, is a painful inflammation of the roots of the sensory nerves which can manifest in any part of the body. The typical, painful skin rash that develops shortly thereafter the pain in the affected area, outlines the pathway of the affected nerve or nerves. Traditional medicine explains how this is caused by a herpes virus, closely related, if not identical, to the varicella or chicken pox virus. However, it does not affect children primarily, but rather adults or older people with an already weakened immune system.

When we get older and experience stressful times are we likely to become victims of the herpes zoster virus? Where and how does our responsibility for our own state of health, as emphasized before, fit in? Are there any specific mental and emotional patterns that will draw the lesson of this illness to us?

A few case histories will help us find some answers:

1) Vanessa, an elementary school teacher, 55 years old and single, is having difficulty coping with the increasing demands of her job –– more children in her classes, more meetings, more reports and no financial compensation to balance this. In the free time she has left, her demanding mother wants to be taken shopping or to her many doctors' appointments. After 4 months of both these pressures, Vanessa came down with a severe attack of shingles, forcing her to rest completely for several months.

2) Faye, a fashion magazine editor, loses her job due to reorganization. While she has the means to support herself for several years, she worries continuously about having no income. Plus she worries about getting older, while she is waiting for the man, whose mistress she has been for several years, to keep his promise about leaving his wife for her. After 6 months of this very frustrating situation, she is diagnosed with shingles.

3) Ingrid, a 62 year old single lady, works hard as an assistant to a very busy hairdresser in a renowned salon. She finds herself getting more tired at work than before and is afraid of becoming unable to meet the demands at work and consequently losing her job. Shortly thereafter, her mother becomes sick and moves in with her in need of care. Ingrid then came down with shingles.

Is the herpes zoster virus lying in wait for all older adults who experience a stressful period in their lives? I believe that there is a much more specific mental and emotional pattern that creates candidates for this illness. Vanessa, Faye and Ingrid all lived in a state of chronic anxiety, irritation and frustration, feeling overwhelmed by the demands of their environment and intense financial worries. We find a very definite lack of receiving nurturing in each of their lives. Apparently this energy pattern has a direct and specific effect on the immune system. It makes people particularly vulnerable to this illness –– the body is using this virus as a vehicle to express the pain of the soul that feels trapped and overwhelmed in this way. The therapeutic consequences of these insights are obvious. In addition to adequate care of the body, self-nurturing initiatives and guidance are needed to shift the mental and emotional focus, and actually lift it up from its victimized state of entrapment to a more spiritual focus in life, not dominated by worry and fear.

Actually, of our 3 case histories, Vanessa did have a good spiritual awareness; however, she felt trapped in her sense of responsibility and service. Faye was trying to apply spiritual teachings to her life, without being able yet to reap results in the form of more inner peace and acceptance of her life's lessons. Ingrid was not yet very aware of spiritual things.

Getting help in developing a set of spiritual insights that we can get to work for us in our daily lives will indeed lift us from our self-imposed hell of fear, anxiety, worry and pain, into the heavenly realms of peace. Essential here is the awareness that we need to develop the faith that we will have all of our needs met as soon as we ask, with true awareness of our worthiness to receive from the joyful abundance of God's Universe, with our minds unclouded by guilt or doubts, and unafraid to make changes which will allow us to receive these things.

As we relax in this awareness, our immune system can strengthen and heal, and so will our entire body, ending any resonance with the pain of shingles.

Peace be with you!

Room for ideas on how you can overcome <u>your</u> worries, fears and any sense of victimization.

CHAPTER 11

ON DIABETES AND THE SWEETNESS OF LIFE

It is generally acknowledged at this time, even by practitioners of allopathic medicine, that there are certain forms of human disease, called psychosomatic, where continuous mental and emotional pressures lead to physical disorders like migraine headaches, stomach ulcers or colitis. In most other forms of human illness however, where such a correlation is not so clearly understood, it is considered not to be there at all. This is based upon our contemporary medical thinking that the human body is, as Dr. Deepak Chopra ironically defined it, "a machine that has somehow learned to think." In this machine, there are parts that can wear out or start malfunctioning, leading to a need for replacement or, if that is not possible, removal as long as this is compatible with life.

Since our doctors tell us that this is just the way it is (and we know that they have studied for many years to gain this knowledge) we believe them and submit ourselves to whatever they tell us to do or to have done to us.

However, in any kind of spiritual study, we are constantly reminded that we create our own reality and that we create our physical health or disease with our own thoughts and feelings. If this is really true, how does this apply to a difficult chronic disease that is not in the psychosomatic group like diabetes mellitus? We all know that this is caused by a pancreas malfunction; meaning that it does not produce enough insulin to maintain a normal sugar metabolism; the sugar (glucose) cannot get into our cells, but remains in the blood and is lost with the urine. This process causes initial symptoms such as weakness, weight loss, excessive thirst and urination. On a long term basis, we find recurrent infections and an acceleration of the aging process.

A different, milder form of diabetes is found in adults who are overweight and who take in too much sugar for the pancreas to handle. This form can often be controlled by diet alone, which is not possible with the first kind.

How could we ever create such a problem through our mind. Well, consider this. We come into this earth plane with certain needs. We need to be loved and nurtured, especially in our childhood and, at any age, we need to experience enough joy––the sweetness of life. This gives us enthusiasm and a motivation to go on and to continue learning our earthly lessons. If there is not enough love, not enough nurturing, not enough sweetness in life, then we perceive emotionally that there isn't any sweetness to life, that there is just work, hardship, responsibility, discipline etc., and then we will subconsciously or even consciously resent life. As our body symbolically expresses what we want or what we do not want, just as we can lose our hearing if we are unwilling to listen to others, we will also shut down our ability to digest the sweetness in life, our sugar, if we feel there is no sweetness to life.

Here is an example of how it works. Mildred, a beautiful young lady, had always been very healthy, and being a model she had an exciting life style which she enjoyed very much. Then she married Steve, who was a very nice and sensitive man; but in their marriage he became an alcoholic, who became abusive and violent when drunk. After ten years of this, during which she had to physically defend herself and her two children many times against him and also had to raise the two children as well as work, the diabetes manifested in a very severe form. When she first came to see me, she had struggled with this illness for 10 years. Yet she understood from my explanations, that what her doctor had been telling her about her illness, that she would have it all her life, and that she would die from its complications, might not necessarily be true. When she learned about the true underlying mechanism of her quite understandable resentment against all the duties and all the responsibility she had had to take on, she understood and could then start working hard at undoing and overcoming this.

Now, how can this be done? Is it really possible to overcome diabetes? It is certainly not easy and it will not happen overnight. But since it has usually taken many years to build the resentment, the protest against the lack of love, nurturing and support, it will also probably take years to create a new mental and emotional perception of life on earth that will heal an illness of this nature. We do need a spiritual focus. We do need to understand that we were never true victims of whatever difficult life circumstances we had to live through, but that we always created those circumstances ourselves for a reason, usually out of guilt over our past actions, sometimes related to past lifetimes.

So diabetics need to give top priority to rediscovering the sweetness in life by pursuing what brings them joy and affirm their worthiness to receive God's abundance in this lifetime, to love and be loved, and to support and be supported. They will be required to let go of all judgments and to apply this understanding in faith, not allowing any doubts to enter. Counseling, various healing treatments and, in certain cases, regressions to uncover past life interactions related to the present life difficulties may be helpful here.

Again, it will not be easy, but it will be most rewarding and lead to much more than just restoring insulin production. We can experience tremendous soul growth in the process and rediscover that God indeed never punishes us with this illness or any other, but is just allowing us to move through it to learn the consequences of focusing elsewhere rather than on His eternal and limitless love. So start to work on this right now –– what else could be more important or worthwhile? Know that He will rejoice in our healing as we were always meant to be healthy and have joy in our life.

CHAPTER 12

CANDIDA ALBICANS AS A LITTLE WHITE LIGHTWORKER

Candida albicans, the most common form of yeast, has only since the late nineteen-seventies and almost exclusively in holistic medical circles been recognized as an important causative factor in human illness. It expresses itself in a variety of common symptoms which indicate malfunctioning of the central nervous system (fatigue, depression, instability, short attention span) or of the digestive system (food allergies, indigestion, bloating) as well as the respiratory and urogenital tracts, among which vaginitis is especially common.

How can a simple little yeast which has been symbiotic with animal and human life for millions of years (which means that it is meant to live in harmony with its hosts, just as lactobacillus acidophilus does in our intestines) suddenly create, in our time, such a mess in our bodies? Has it turned from a friend into an enemy? Or could it be that we have not kept our part of the agreement for joyful and harmonious cooperation and coexistence?

To find the answer to this question let us look at some factors that create a predisposition for yeast infection as it is commonly and mistakenly called. As the yeast is supposed to be there, it is not really an infection but rather an overgrowth. These causative factors are known to be: use of antibiotics, especially prolonged or recurrent use, such is often the case with acne treatments; use of cortisone and oral contraceptives; ongoing mental and emotional pressures and frustrations; and last but not least, the all American diet with its chocolate-chip cookies, 32 kinds of ice cream and a whole range of other ways to take in refined sugar.

It is not hard to understand how all these predisposing factors, which appear to be accepted if not integral ingredients of our 21st century American life-style, lead us away from harmony, balance and good health. Antibiotics destroy our healthy intestinal flora, create overgrowth of either other bacteria or yeast, and can cause severe allergic or toxic reactions. Cortisone and other synthetic hormones upset our delicate and complex hormonal balance. Mental and emotional pressures or stress create biochemical changes that weaken our immune system. Refined sugars do that too, plus they are the ideal food for yeast, inviting it to overgrow even more.

So would it be correct to observe that this little yeast cell, Candida albicans, is sounding the alarm, indicating that some important changes have to be made for the body's health or even survival, rather than being the villain, attacking an innocent victim? I would definitely think so.

Let us look at the name Candida albicans. My Latin dictionary defines "albicans" as whitemaker. Candidus (fem. candida) means blinding white, snow-white, or sometimes, radiating a heavenly brilliance. Whoever gave this little fungus this beautiful name must have had some intuitive awareness of the fact that we are definitely dealing with a friend here, not with an enemy, and that this friend is committed to keeping us from creating too much of a mess in our body or it will intervene, showing us that what we are doing to our body is not at all conducive to our physical health, or even our mental, emotional or spiritual health! Our little friend is in this way behaving like a little teacher who says, "Stop right here! See what you have done to yourself! It is time now to rebalance! Shift your physical, mental and emotional diet back to where I feel comfortable with you again and you with me!"

It is obviously impossible to discuss here in depth the diagnosis and treatment of Candidiasis or yeast overgrowth, as this could easily fill a book in itself as demonstrated by William C. Crook, M.D. in his excellent book, "The Yeast Connection."

My focus in this chapter is primarily to show that when we are diagnosed with a yeast "infection", taking fungicide drugs such as are available at this time, is not the ideal way of meeting this challenge. We need to heed the message, accept our responsibility for having created this lesson, and face the music by giving priority to all the necessary steps, through our diet and other changes in our life style, which will bring back health and balance to our body and which will be answered by our little white lightworkers inside with a smile and a "Thank you! We knew you could do it! Now let us play and have fun together again!"

How have you been treating <u>your</u> Candida albicans? Is there room for improvement?

CHAPTER 13

SOME REFLECTIONS ON CANCER THERAPY

People who are diagnosed with cancer and do not believe in the principles of holistic medicine and also do not believe in God, nor in the spiritual concept that we are responsible for our own health, usually do not have any problem choosing their cancer therapy. They will most likely follow their doctor's suggestion to undergo surgery, chemotherapy and/or radiation therapy without any hesitation. Maybe they will get well again. And if they do not, they will nevertheless feel that they fought the disease with all available means.

In working with people who are diagnosed with cancer who do believe in holistic medicine, in God and in spiritual laws, I find that they are often torn between the different options that are available to them. Their diagnosis will most likely have been made or confirmed by a traditional M.D. who will put pressure on them to follow the only treatment system in which he believes. And in view of the fact that making the right choice is most likely a matter of life and death here, they find their spiritual belief system tested to the limit. It may not be hard for someone with a number of years experience in meditation and prayer to go within and ask if they should make the job change or relationship change they are contemplating and receive the answer with sufficient clarity. But when you have to go within and ask whether you should accept the verdict of a mastectomy, chemotherapy and/or radiation for a suspect lump in your breast, then it can be very hard to hear God's answer to your question and trust it, especially if you hear that you would not have to go through that ordeal if other options were used.

In a situation like this, it is very helpful to contemplate the true causative levels and move away from the feeling of being the victim of some kind of curse over which the spiritual principles that we try to apply to our lives have no power. As stated before, there is no disease or illness that truly originates at the physical level. We create or build with our mind our physical reality, whether that be health or illness. If we have created an imbalance that is expressed as a physical illness, then we must understand that the physical illness is our body's message to us that we need first to make the necessary changes to restore and heal the imbalance, after which physical healing can follow. The changes in our mental and emotional attitude that we need to make to heal ourselves from physical illness are usually very specific. Louise Hay, in her classic book "You can heal your life", and Carolyn Myss, in her book "Anatomy of the Spirit" have both provided "checklists", where we can look up our illness and find what it is that we need to work on.

In the case of cancer, it is very important that we do not allow ourselves to be caught up in the fear that our allopathic physicians may try to instill in us if we do not blindly follow what they tell us to do. This would leave us totally without any power to actively participate in our healing process. But if we accept our responsibility for having created our illness, even if it is cancer (possibly from harboring a deep sorrow, a strong resentment or bitterness for a number of years), then we can also accept and claim our power to make a change, to get to work right away and get help in overcoming and clearing from our subconscious mind the old issues that created the damage. Then there will be nothing helpless about us anymore and we will be actively in charge of our self-healing process. We may still need the assistance of our allopathic oncologist to a degree, but only to the extent that feels right when we meditate and pray about it. This may mean that we only accept a part of his suggested therapeutic program. In working this way, we realize that the greatest healing tool that we have available to us is not our oncologist's assortment of chemotherapy and radiation, but rather the divine chemotherapy and radiation that we can and should expose ourselves to daily in meditation, flooding ourselves with golden healing light that, with perseverance, will erase and transmute whatever the deep pains were that led to the creation of the illness.

Thus we make God our primary physician, in charge of the total team of helpers with which we surround ourselves. Our team may include, in addition to our traditional oncologist, a holistic physician who is experienced in alternative cancer therapy and nutrition counseling, a spiritual healer who can help draw the divine healing energies to us and a massage therapist to aid the body in its recovery and release of toxins. In this way, we can move through the lesson of cancer, no longer dominated by fear. We can demonstrate to ourselves, to others and especially to the traditional medical community of our time, that by applying the spiritual laws that we know, by seeking a better mental and emotional balance and by calling on the department of divine chemotherapy and radiation, the results are more than worth trying. They may well lead us through a healing experience that will, when completed, make us realize that our life has been enriched rather than damaged by it. And, as the ultimate reward, by going through this lesson we will probably grow closer to God.

Room to reflect on <u>your</u> responsibility towards your body, and how you can work to clear any negative attitudes that, with time, will damage your body if you don't do this work <u>now</u>.

CHAPTER 14

ON HEALING A HEALER'S HIPS

With regard to maintaining or restoring our physical health, there is an obvious advantage to having the spiritual awareness that we are responsible for our own state of health as we ultimately create it through our own mind. Acting on this insight can protect us from the aggressive approaches of the medical establishment of this time, e.g. when surgery is recommended for chronic degenerative disease. Can this same awareness also create an impediment to our healing? My answer is definitely yes, as is illustrated by the following case history.

Tom, a healer from Poland, came to see me after hesitating for almost a year to seek help. He had undergone hip replacement surgery on one hip about ten years before, after the joint had been damaged by several accidents. Now he was struggling with the reality that his other hip was gradually giving him more pain and difficulty when he walked. As his hip surgery had required over a year of painful convalescence, Tom was not eager to go through this again. However, now that he had been trained as a Reiki healer and teacher, this problem was interfering with this ability to work. Moreover, it was intensified somewhat by a sense of incompetence. He felt that this should not have happened to him as he should exemplify health and wholeness. At least, he felt that he should have been able to heal himself once this condition developed. These contemplations had led him to delay seeking help for his suffering for a long time.

Tom's eyes were kind and gentle, but showed a lot of pain. It seemed obvious that we needed to check into his past to find out how the mental and emotional root causes for his condition were laid down. Tom had not been a happy child. He remembered that since his arrival on earth he felt lost here, and always wanted to "go home" even though he had no idea where that home was. He also knew that he could not ask his parents or his brother, as they would not have understood. His mother was some 25 years younger than his father and had raised her two children almost by herself, for her husband did not want to be bothered. She ruled with discipline rather than with love and kindness and could have a bad temper. She would beat Tom after he broke some kind of house rule and then instill guilt in him by saying, "Look what you made me do!" Thus he could not even express his anger over this kind of treatment. For Tom, who is a Capricorn with Leo rising, not a Sagittarius as the double hip problem might have led the astrologers among you to expect, this was a very difficult challenge and gave him even more reason for not wanting to be here. He loved to go to sleep –– that was as close to going home as he could get! But then the next day he was back in his earth prison. He decided that the safest thing for him to do was to just sit still and not move. He concluded that movement somehow eventually led to punishment. Through a regression technique the adult Tom was amazed to get back in touch with the power of his inner child's decision not to move, which had for many years as subconscious thought and feeling energy, quite successfully attacked his body's apparatus for movement –– the hips. He could see this very clearly now, and also how all the anger that he had never been allowed to express had added fuel to the fire. But now he could start releasing the powerful contents of his subconscious mind that had affected him so strongly. Of course Tom would also need chiropractic work, massage, a gentle exercise program diet advice, vitamin and mineral supplements and homeopathic remedies. But releasing his destructive subconscious beliefs would be most essential to his successful completion of the healing process.

There are two things that we can learn from this: firstly, let us not underestimate the severity of hip replacement surgery. The orthopedic surgeon may speak lightly of it, but he does not feel the pain that his patient suffers for a long time after surgery. Secondly, we must even as healers not demand of ourselves that we heal ourselves at all times. This would require us to be capable of looking into our own subconscious mind, which is very hard to do. It is good that, as healers and teachers, we want to be examples of good health, harmony and balance. But after all, the earth plane is a dimension where we are all striving for perfection without having yet attained it fully. Maybe we will eventually learn to change our response to disease which manifests in our body from anger, denial, resentment and frustration or even guilt, and be willing to listen to our body's message or even acknowledge the reality that there is a mental or emotional imbalance that now needs our attention, so we can work on eliminating its root cause. In this manner we will take another step toward attaining the perfection of the Christ consciousness, which is ultimately attainable for all of us. But let us be gentle and patient with ourselves and with each other while we are doing this work. Let us also be willing to accept each other's help, so we can find and work on our blind spots. And let us also realize that working through any illness is a very meaningful aspect of a healer's training, as he or she will always be more compassionate and understanding with any patient who presents himself or herself later with that or a similar disease. Overcoming an illness in this way can be like having an additional degree in healing qualities, enabling the healer to give an even higher level of service to our family of Man.

How well are you able to accept and seek help for <u>your</u> physical challenges? Make some plans.

CHAPTER 15

THE CASE OF THE SULKING SEEKER

When we begin to shift our focus in life from the primary cycles of working, eating, sleeping and expressing our sexuality, into a greater awareness of spiritual laws, and we start to consciously apply these laws in our daily lives, we tend to have an expectation that God will reward our efforts with a happier, healthier life with less problems to deal with because we are now more "in tune" with our earthly environment and our higher guidance.

Well, as many of us have come to realize, very often it does not seem to work that way. Instead, our life appears to get more chaotic and stressful when we start to work on ourselves in this way. This may lead to great discouragement, turning away from "the path" or blaming God for letting us down.

Apparently, it is hard for us to understand that when we start to refine and raise our vibrational energy, we are no longer able to resonate as well as before with coarser energy patterns of other people, food and drinks, or even our own thoughts, without getting ourselves in trouble, while we were quite comfortable with them before. This means that our soul is expressing through our body what it needs now and what it does not want anymore. Let me illustrate this.

Sandra, a sweet housewife and mother of three young children in her mid-thirties, had consulted me a number of times in her efforts to overcome issues of sexual abuse in childhood, issues of over-disciplinary parental programming and marital problems. After she distinctly improved for some time, her next visit started with an outburst of tears, indicating a big depression over the fact that in spite of several years of work on herself, she was still tired most of the time and struggling with an ongoing throat infection, a vaginal yeast infection and painful knees. I knew her as a sensitive and quite spiritually-oriented person who had been quite capable at previous sessions of getting in touch with her higher guidance and obtaining strength and inspiration from there. After a stress-release treatment and balancing of her chakras, Sandra felt much better and was again able to get some very meaningful answers from her inner guidance to questions that I suggested she ask, e.g. regarding the deeper meaning of her physical ailments. Thus she heard that behind her throat problem was a tendency to hold back expressing herself out of fear of other people's judgments; she especially had problems expressing her dissatisfaction about anything in the presence of her dominant parents-in-law.

Her vaginal yeast infection was related to anger, mostly toward her husband for being so preoccupied with his successful business that he was not really there for the children and when he was home, he tried to mold them into his idea of perfection rather than expressing love and affection toward them. Another part of the anger, focused in the sexual arena, was still related to the old sexual abuse issues. And finally she heard the word "intolerance" as being the mental energy that kept her knees from healing. They were the focus of expression for certain rigid or inflexible and judgmental outlooks on life she had not yet been able to overcome for they were a part of early parental programming, subconsciously still active.

She could now understand that her ailments were not an expression of God's cruelty, nor of His ignoring the spiritual work she had been doing, but rather that her body was expressing strong messages; it had become so much more sensitive due to years of more conscious eating habits and inner spiritual work that it was no longer able or willing to be a storehouse for those energies of fear, anger and judgment of which she was not even aware.

These insights gave her a lot of hope, encouragement and even enthusiasm to work toward completely overcoming these root causes for her physical ailments. She could see that her ailments, for which she had strongly blamed her body before, were in truth more like teachers, demonstrating clearly in which areas more refining and raising of mental and emotional vibrational energy was required. Thus she could also let go of her resentment toward the people in her life who were not at all working on themselves, who did all the wrong things, expressed lots of ugly thoughts and yet appeared to be healthy. She realized the principle of "Noblesse oblige"; when all the souls' vibrations are still unrefined, they can still be in some kind of balance, but this would definitely not be a balance for her.

In summary, while working to improve our attitudes in life, when we find ourselves sulking or resentful about our seemingly blocked progress, we need to turn within and be willing to hear the messages we have been ignoring. Sometimes we may need some help with this. But this approach can bring about such powerful transformation in our perceptions about ourselves in this dimension of illusions called the earth plane, that I feel we all need to work with it. So "Man, know thyself," and rise above the sulking seeker's syndrome.

Room for a short note to God on how <u>you</u> have felt let down by Him in the past, and how you feel now about your progress on your life path.

CHAPTER 16

ON HIDING YOUR LIGHT UNDER A BUSHEL

Hiding your light under a bushel feels like such a dumb thing to do that no one would ever consider it. And yet we have all done it. Most of us are still doing it all the time and we do not even realize when or how. It will always interfere with our spiritual growth and expansion, or our empowerment, whenever we let it happen. So what is really going on here? How does it work?

Example one: Jordan is 25 years old, with chronic fatigue attributed to the Epstein-Barr virus. He is still living with his parents who love him very much and whom he loves very much too. Jordan is very talented in the creative arts: he is a talented pianist, a good ballet dancer, and has won several acting contests. He would love to become an actor; however, his parents are very strongly against these plans and insist that he pursue a career with more financial security, such as medicine or law. He is afraid of the idea of losing the support and love of his parents. He also knows that he would not enjoy burying himself in a career that provides him no inspiration of any kind. Thus he finds himself trapped in a very frustrating conflict that has, with time, paralyzed him mentally and emotionally.

This conflict has expressed itself in the physical body as some kind of paralysis of the immune system resulting in a susceptibility to the Epstein-Barr virus. The symbolic message of a disease of this kind is always that we must focus on the mental and emotional issues of a "paralyzing" nature from which we feel unable to break away.

What does this example have to do with light and bushels? Let me explain. The divine light that we are, contains and expresses the divine spark, the creative spirit that we are, and the divine love and joy that we resonate with and radiate out from ourselves. The saints and great spiritual teachers could always be recognized by the light that could be seen around them, as was constantly the case with Jesus. This light can be seen by normal people not just clairvoyants.

Hiding our light under a bushel means, in fact, any action we take which diminishes or obstructs the flow of divine love, light and inspiration through us and out into the world. Jordan's inability to choose to develop his natural gifts and talents was based upon his love for his parents, as he did not want to disappoint them, mixed with the fear of losing his parents' love for him. As these feelings may remain mostly at subconscious levels, it can be very difficult to deal with them adequately.

Jordan came to me asking for help with improving his physical energy and stamina. I gave him healing treatments, reviewed his use of vitamin and mineral supplements, and recommended a good Aloe Vera concentrate to strengthen his immune system. But probably of greatest importance here was that I explained to him the dynamics that had resulted in the manifestation of his illness.

He responded well. His energy level went up within the first week. After five weeks he had the strength to tell his parents that he had chosen to pursue his acting career. He has since overcome his illness completely, while traditional contemporary medicine says there is no cure for this illness caused by the Epstein-Barr virus.

Example two: this experience was remembered by one of my friends who saw herself as a baby in a cradle, hungry and tired, crying, if not screaming, to be fed. After quite some time her mother charged into the room very angry about the crying, which manifested as a very unappealing cloud of coarse crimson color around her. As this was not the first time this happened, my friend as this baby decided she did not want to see any more of these ugly colors, so she shut down her gift of clairvoyance, which would only come back to her after much inner work some thirty years later.

So there are several, if not many, ways to hide our light, to limit ourselves in our efforts not to lose love, not to have to perceive ugliness, or to make ourselves fit better into a group of people who get us to believe that in order to be normal and healthy we have to think, feel and be just like them. We can all fill in our own examples of how we have done this many times and in many ways. Let us not judge ourselves for this, as we have all learned what happens to us when we use these techniques of reducing ourselves. However, now is the time to stop hiding our light, reducing, limiting and disempowering ourselves! In order to free ourselves from these mechanisms, all we need to do is to start applying the very simple basics common to all spiritual teaching: love God, love yourself, love all others, and do not judge. But in order to do this we have to stop resonating with the vast reservoirs of judgment and blame (including self-judgment and self-blame), doubt and fear, that are at this time like enormous clouds hanging over our entire planet in the mental and emotional realms.

Let us realize that it is considered normal to judge and to blame, and to be in fear, thus practicing denial of love. How can horror films be as popular as they are in America, if we the people do not enjoy resonating with these energies? So, the price we pay for breaking away from that pattern when we start building our light and empowering ourselves again by developing more of our divine potential is that we give up being normal. Let us realize here that we are probably already abnormal as we are reading a book of this kind!

I can tell you from personal experience that it is extremely rewarding to become more aware of all these energy patterns that shut down our heart chakra, or in other words, reduce our ability to resonate with divine love. Feel what reading a "normal" newspaper, watching the news on TV or denying someone help does to the flow of love and light through your heart energy center, and then make up your mind as to whether or not that is how you wish to be. And if you do not enjoy that sense of shutting down, of denying love, then use that as your motivation to stop reducing yourself, hiding your light, and using your bushels in the wrong manner.

Enjoy just the reverse and become the light of the world. Once you begin, you will feel God's blessings upon you, as well as those from our planet Earth, which remains in dire straits as long as you do not start. So get with it!

CHAPTER 17

SOME REFLECTIONS ON CHILD ABUSE

As astrologers explain to us, this is a time of great activity for Pluto, that far out, slow-moving little Scorpionic fighter in the astrological arena, specializing in uncovering or exposing nasty aspects of truth that were quite successfully hidden before.

The surge in attention that the issue of child abuse is receiving at this time is undoubtedly related to this Plutonic energy; as well as to the fact that the collective consciousness of humanity has been slowly but steadily rising in recent years, which has found expression in more initiatives to protect more children as well as animals from abuse.

So how do we deal with this issue while struggling as we are in our daily lives to apply more of the spiritual teachings that we have absorbed?

Are we allowing ourselves to resonate with the majority of the people who scream for Old Testament forms of punishment, like removing body parts of the offenders? We probably feel that this is not really the way to deal with this.

On the other hand, this is indeed quite a challenge for us in our attempts to be non-judgmental, especially those of us who are at this time working hard to overcome child abuse issues ourselves. Here are some aspects that may be helpful to contemplate:

1) We are learning in our spiritual studies that we need to replace the concept of the helpless victim and the cruel perpetrator with the concept that an agreement is made between two souls to go through an experience which will lead to important learning and soul wisdom. Through our experience with past life regressions, we are learning that there is often a role reversal between the victim and the perpetrator in subsequent incarnations which provides the complete learning experience for each one of the two souls involved in this exchange. (This applies to many types of violent behavior, even murder.) Would we not be inclined to think differently about a sex offender of a young child, if we knew that at the soul level this child had given him permission to do just that to have this learning experience? Or if we knew that the child had reversed the roles with this offender in a past lifetime?

2) Imagine this scenario. After a series of group incarnations in which three souls have been

husband, wife and daughter, now they change their arrival times on the planet in such a way that the soul who was the wife before is now the daughter and vice versa, while the father remained in his old role. Each one of these souls has strong emotional body-memories of past relationships. Therefore, the sexual interaction between the husband and wife (former daughter) is likely to suffer from the feeling that something is not quite right, while there may be a strong sexual attraction between father and daughter (former wife), which the father finds himself acting upon against his will.

In light of all these possible aspects, which are invariably hidden from our view, we may better understand why God tells us time and again –– Judgment is Mine. In other words, there are too many aspects to these situations that you are not aware of, so do not even try to assess what is right or wrong here.

Seeing situations in this way has definitely helped me not to judge other people too strongly any more in their interactions, even if they are abusive. And let us not think that we are so far above and beyond abusive behavior. If we are, we probably are because we have already moved through that kind of learning in the past, and we no longer need that experience.

People who have developed a spiritual focus and awareness are obviously better able to work through child abuse issues than "normal people," who are still caught up in "normal people's" judgments and resentments. Spiritual seekers understand that the only way to explain such behavior is to apply their understanding of a greater concept, like that of reincarnation, and to accept at the soul level, the experience they went through. They are also much more open to the very effective techniques that are available to them of releasing the cellular memories of those abusive events, through regression techniques into early childhood, or even past lifetimes if necessary. For example, the memories of sexual abuse that are often stored in the reproductive organs themselves, can thus be remembered, re-experienced and released with breathing techniques that involve color visualizations. In this way, blockages in present-time adult sexual enjoyment can be removed, sometimes in a short time, and sometimes it takes considerably longer.

So, if Plutonic energy pushed the child abuse victims, who are now adults, into working through these issues and successfully releasing them, leading them to much more enjoyment and fulfillment in their present lives, then I would expect them to agree with me that it has all been worth it. And that Divine Intelligence was actually working behind this Plutonic push urging them to leave behind their limited judgmental views and attitudes, accept the learning, apply greater understanding and forgiveness, and grow into a stronger resonance with and expression of the Light of God that we have always carried within. So let it shine and enjoy the precious gift that life on earth is.

Room to express <u>your</u> thoughts on child abuse here; do you need to work on them?

CHAPTER 18

SOME REFLECTIONS FOR SPIRITUAL SMOKERS

The majority of people who are on the spiritual path and who are also smokers are not particularly proud of it. They usually feel some degree of guilt about mistreating their body in this way and a sense of not having enough strength to stop. "One day I'll be strong enough to stop" and so the habit continues.

On the other hand, there is a much smaller category of people who have in their spiritual studies come across the theme that our physical reality does not create our belief systems, but to the contrary, our belief systems create our physical reality. So they say, we can smoke for we believe that our body is able to dispose of all the toxic by-products and waste of smoking without being affected by them. While I acknowledge the power of the mind over the body, I still feel that they give their body a lot of unnecessary work to do. Yet I realize that my little judgment is totally irrelevant to them.

So, with or without guilt, why do spiritual people smoke? We all know that physical addictions usually meet a need to escape from the harshness, the pain and the suffering that can be a part of our physical experience. While alcohol and recreational drugs offer a temporary escape from emotional pain, smoking offers sensitive people the following:

1) The benefit of reducing their sensitivity and the related nervousness they have when trying to function in a rather insensitive, noisy or tense environment. E.g. one of my dear friends, a flight controller at Sky Harbor airport and a very spiritual and sensitive person, has only recently after many years gathered the courage, strength and spiritual insights to make it possible for her to stop smoking at her job, which is by definition, a high-stress environment. Some people say they feel the need to smoke to ground themselves. I would be inclined to include that aspect in this same category.

2) Like drinking and overeating, smoking can, to a degree, cover up anger; it will still be there, but more in the background and not felt so much.

3) When we have, for whatever reasons, developed a sense of low self-esteem, we will subconsciously be inclined to find ways to confirm that as our truth; I am unable to overcome my addiction to smoking, so I am right not to value myself.

At this point we can probably agree that nicotine is not a very good psychotherapist. So if we could contemplate a new effort to stop smoking, what avenues for help are available?

1) On the physical level, the addiction can gradually be overcome with the help of a "nicotine patch" program, available through family physicians. In my experience, allergies to these patches develop in only a minority of cases. However, this program will need to be combined with some of the following avenues of help.

2) Acupuncture –– Since our meridians interact strongly with our autonomous nervous system, it can be a meaningful support system. It is also possible that the use of magnets, strategically placed, would be helpful but I have no personal experience in this area.

3) Hypnotherapy –– This is another powerful way to have our mental and emotional programs changed.

4) Healing and counseling sessions are very powerful in addressing the emotional dependency, making us more aware of our inner emotional attitudes and enabling us to adjust them as needed, shedding our limited belief systems in the process. E.g. anger is very often based upon a judgmental attitude, which can be transformed through counseling; we can learn to allow other people as well as ourselves to still be imperfect at this time and thus develop a new attitude of forgiveness

and compassion. The causes of low self-esteem can be found and healed. We can develop a new sense of self-confidence and worthiness to have a good time here on earth, rather than attracting limitations through a sense of non-deserving.

5) Again on the physical level –– as far as over-sensitivity to our sometimes harsh surroundings is concerned, a healthy diet, a good exercise program, enough sleep, and the daily practice of breathing exercises and meditation will give our nervous system so much more strength that we will be able to function as an island of stability in any stormy environment.

We all struggle in our own way with the divine commandment not to judge. Nonsmokers tend to judge smokers, especially in spiritual circles, and smokers may tend to judge their judges for they feel they have the right to make their own decisions, which of course, they do. In other words, these reflections are not designed primarily to criticize the smokers among us, but I hope to give those among us who smoke and who have tried or contemplated quitting, but have not felt strong enough, some additional tools with which to build more strength. And it is to them that I say: "Try again! You can do it this time! God is with you and good luck!"

What addictions do <u>you</u> have to work on? Make some notes on how to start.

CHAPTER 19

WHY WOULD WE NOT WANT TO BE HEALERS?

When I was told in 1977 that I had the potential to become a healer as well as a doctor, I had two emotional responses move through me. The first one was positive; of course it was flattering to my ego, plus I already had had a sense about that deep down inside. The second one was, however, uncomfortable; I did not know why.

Much later, in 1991, in a series of past life regressions at Chris Griscom's Light Institute in Galisteo, New Mexico, I was assisted in remembering a lifetime in Germany in the 16th century where I was a monk living in a monastery. I got back in touch with a strong deep-rooted feeling of unworthiness as I had been unable to keep my vow of celibacy in that lifetime. That made me feel like a total failure in the eyes of God, as I imagined Him at that time. Even though at the time of this regression I had already been involved with healing work for quite a few years, remembering and releasing that cellular memory pattern of unworthiness was very helpful to me for it enabled me to bring through more and stronger healing energy.

So this feeling of unworthiness can be one reason that would stop us from getting wholeheartedly involved in channeling healing energy. There is another reason that comes up many times in past life regression, i.e., the bad if not horrible experiences that people had to go through in the past, such as in the Dark Ages, when they got involved with healing work. These experiences would make them determined never to fall into this trap again!

Here are some examples: The first time I came upon this theme was in 1985 in Holland. I was still working as an ear, nose and throat specialist and was trying with all I knew to cure a chronic bilateral ear infection of a female patient in her late thirties. I was unsuccessful. Luckily she decided to consult a healer, who told her that her ear infection was a symbolic expression of her strong resistance against developing her sense of clairaudience, as a part of her soul urge to be a healer again in this lifetime. The last time she had been a healer she ended up being cruelly tortured and killed in one of the many witch trials that took place during the Middle Ages throughout Europe. She had promised herself then never again to get involved with this stuff! I remember that I was deeply impressed with this explanation for why the ear infection could not be cured without resolving the underlying conflict. Needless to say, after she understood and released her resistance, her ears cleared up. I trust that this lady has been actively and happily involved in healing work since then.

Another example: A dear friend of mine, who had been a successful businesswoman, felt drawn to get involved with healing work a few years ago. As this healing work grew in intensity, she suddenly began experiencing severe pain in both hands when she was giving healing treatments. She had the awareness that a past life regression might shed some light on this and it did. She remembered that she had been punished in a past lifetime for doing healing work by having her hands held in a fire!

So these subconscious memory patterns can be big stumbling blocks on our path to becoming or perfecting ourselves as healers, as long as we avoid dealing with them. There may be several other reasons why people do not let themselves become healers. I find the themes of unworthiness and bad experiences in this line of work to be most predominant. And, with either one, once we bring these themes to our conscious awareness, for which regression therapy can be a very effective tool, then overcoming them can be so simple. With the theme of unworthiness, we know now that God is not the Old Testament type of angry, jealous and judgmental God. We know now that God's unconditional love forgives us in the same moment that we act in any way for which we would judge ourselves. Applying this knowledge we can strive to develop an unconditionally loving attitude toward ourselves as He has. With the theme of bad experiences in the past, we know that times are different now. The

Middle Ages and its many witch trials through which most, if not all, healers have suffered is now behind us. We can look ahead into this golden dawn of the Millennium of Peace, where all healers are asked, or rather strongly urged, to take their place in the active healing work force, assisting the entire human family in their preparation for the glorious times ahead.

So if you feel you could be part of this work force, but have not yet stepped forward, do so now! Allow yourself to be drawn into whatever healing classes or seminars that speak to you most strongly. And know that while you develop your healing powers, God and the angelic forces smile and breathe a sigh of relief that you are indeed now fulfilling your promise to them, to yourself, and to those who will be needing your help.

Do <u>you</u> have any, possibly deeply hidden, interest in becoming involved in any kind of healing work? And if so, how can you begin to prepare yourself?

CHAPTER 20

MAKE TODAY YOUR LAST JUDGMENT DAY!

O f all the commandments that God gave us, the commandment not to judge (Judgment is Mine) may well be the most violated one to this day and has definitely been a strong causative factor for the retarded pace of spiritual growth that the human family has demonstrated for the past few thousand years.

Actually, we now live in a society that actively encourages or even demands judgments from us. Just take a look at what is considered worthwhile to be shown on TV news or printed on the first page of our newspapers. Murders, any kind of criminal activities and accidents, preferably those involving massive death and damages, and someone who is in some way considered responsible and who can be blamed for it, appears to be the preferred menu. This is intended to invoke reactions like: "The bastard(s)! A good thing we still have the death penalty! Let's use it here!" And, if there is a major natural disaster like another hurricane in Florida, we can judge and blame God, "How could He let this happen to us?"

Apparently we have not yet grasped the meaning, the divine guidance or wisdom that went into God's commandment for us not to judge. But if we look at the effects of judgment and blame (which must include self-judgment and self-blame), we see that there is a lot that is very unattractive about it. E.g., judgment creates great limitations in our thinking patterns in the sense that they result in a rigidity, hardening of our thoughts and feelings or, in other words, of our heart. We feel that the person who we must judge is not worthy of our love. But with this mental and emotional attitude of condemnation, we are creating an undesirable series of changes in our physical body, such as:

1. Rigidity of our spine, which can develop into a true ankylosis with time; our innate flexibility can get lost completely.

2. Limited range of movement and eventually degenerative changes in a joint, like the shoulder, hip or knee, especially if we hold onto anger as well as our judgments.

3. Rigidity in our outlook on life reflects as impairment of our vision. Our need to wear reading glasses when we are in our forties or older, is not a normal aspect of aging. Our body is designed to last even longer than the ages of our first Biblical forefathers, who reached ages of close to 1000 years. So even the hardening of our eye

lens and the immobility of our eye muscles reflects our judgments as well as our unwillingness to see other aspects.

4. Likewise, we think that it is normal to lose our hearing as we get older; it is not and as we all know, it does not happen to everyone. But it will happen to those of us who have crystallized opinions (judgments) about people who are in our lives and to whom we are unwilling to really listen. So, our body will always symbolically shut down functions that we are not using. And there is more.

5. As we harden our heart in our judgments, we prepare for heart disease.

6. By thinking rigid thoughts we harden the arteries in our brain and we prepare for senility, Alzheimer's disease, or a stroke.

Not a very pretty picture is it? Would you agree with me that God knew what He was doing when He ordered us not to judge? Would this list of the effects of a judgmental attitude give you any motivation to do something about your tendency to judge?

Maybe you will say, well I am not sure if I really believe this stuff. If you feel this way, I ask you to consider the people in your life who you know to have a very judgmental attitude and then check out for yourself how well their body is functioning. As it takes time for the many detrimental effects of a judgmental attitude to be fully expressed in the body, you can see this most clearly with people who are about 50 years or older. Consider their flexibility of movement, eyesight and hearing, and if they have any heart condition or blood pressure problem. If you find any positive correlation, use that insight to decide to do something about your tendency to judge right now. Make this day your last judgment day!

You will need another approach, another attitude then to replace the judgmental attitude. Let this be an attitude of acceptance, of allowing everyone to learn their life lessons in whatever way they choose; this must include yourself. Let go of all judgments you have made in this lifetime of yourself, your parents and all others, and accept the learning and the soul wisdom it has brought to you. If you feel incapable of doing that entirely by yourself, seek some help from a healer or counselor who you feel you can trust.

You will feel a tremendous weight being lifted from you as you let go of your judgments and you will feel much younger and more joyful, for judgments bring seriousness, heaviness and lack of joy. You will have a sense that you can feel God's love for you much more clearly because your judgments are no longer interfering with that flow of love into you. As you no longer sow judgments, you no longer reap them. An attitude of allowing others to be who they are and to grow (or not to grow) as they choose, contains the energies of love and forgiveness both. If we, as a human family, learn to shift from a judgmental attitude to one of acceptance, heaven on earth will soon be here. And now, as the long announced earth changes are obviously starting to take place, announcing the beginning of the Aquarian Age, we can see that the planet is not going to stop, but move straight forward into this glorious new era in our evolution. We will have to clean up our act and give up our judgmental attitudes, if we want to stay with her. So let's get with it!

What judgmental attitudes are you aware that <u>you</u> have? Are you ready to start working on allowing the imperfections that are still a part of your life to be there? Make some notes on your primary issues with this.

CHAPTER 21

THE DARK DYNAMICS OF GUILT

Having focused on the general consequences of a judgmental attitude upon our life and particularly our health in the previous chapter, let us now look at a special kind of judgment which holds dramatic consequences for our ability to enjoy our earthly existence. This is, of course, the judgment upon ourselves, commonly called guilt.

Guilt has, along with the other kinds of judgment, been a part of the human experience ever since Adam and Eve ate the forbidden fruit of the Tree of Knowledge of Good and Evil. And even though we are trying to understand that God is showering us all the time with His immense unconditional love, which has to include total forgiveness, we have allowed our collective human consciousness to become totally soaked and saturated with a sense of our sinfulness. Our Christian church fathers have been preaching and hammering into our minds that we are born in sin, live in sin, and die in sin, thus being totally unworthy to ever be in God's presence. We are realizing rather late that these church leaders were working to gain more power and control over us, their followers, instead of bringing us the pure teachings from God as presented through Jesus Christ, who taught us, in John 14:12, "He that believeth in me, the works that I do, shall he do also, and greater works than these shall he do, because I go unto my Father." Is that not a wonderful vote of confidence in us sinners, that we can lift the awful weight of our guilt, rise above it, and start acting like Masters who are aware of their ability to heal themselves and others, and perform miracles through the power of divine love?

Let me provide you with an additional motive to do so. One unfortunate aspect of guilt is that it has creative power like all of our thoughts and feelings. Guilt acts upon the subconscious mind, is stored there, and as it builds up to sufficient intensity, it creates a subconscious need for punishment. It is like practicing black magic upon yourself! For example: a Jewish businessman living in the U.S.A. was involved in a car accident. This happened during the Persian Gulf War, while Saddam's scud missiles were hitting targets in Israel every other day. Since he was aware of his responsibility for his earthly experiences and manifestations, he asked his counselor why he got involved in that stupid accident. When he heard the answer -- that he had felt guilty toward his friends and relatives in Israel who were in constant danger while he was not, and that he had set himself up for a dangerous experience through this guilt —— he had to acknowledge this was true.

I have a dear friend who was born in Germany in the thirties. The many illnesses and physical injuries that she has had to endure in her life can, to a considerable degree, be related to her guilt over being part of a nation that was responsible for inflicting the holocaust upon the Jewish people.

Many times guilt is carried over into next incarnations, manifesting hardship in the form of unloving parents or stepparents, physical diseases or handicaps, or any other kind of hardship which limits experiencing a joyful earthly life. Is it not time now to decide, both individually and collectively, that we have all worked with this scenario more than enough? Why do we not just drop guilt here and now, and start applying God's attitude of unconditional love and forgiveness toward ourselves? We need to declare or affirm that we are now willing to let go of all self-judgment and start loving ourselves as God loves us with no exceptions or conditions of any kind. This may be a bit difficult in the beginning, as our mind tends to keep using circuits of thought that it has always used. You need to monitor your mind here and jump right in when you catch yourself in a "guilt circuit," and guide your thoughts into the new circuits of forgiveness and accept the learning that has taken place, thus maintaining the flow of love toward yourself. If this remains difficult to do, it may be necessary to get professional help, e.g. in the form of counseling, to help you get in touch consciously with any strong sources of guilt that you are carrying in your subconscious mind, which can then be released and healed.

We have to rid ourselves of guilt, as well as release all other judgments of others, if we are to fulfill the promise given us in John 14:12. We need to release these heavier and slower vibrations that we have been carrying around, before we can start resonating with the higher currents of light and divine love and start anchoring these in the earth plane as is so intensely needed at this time. And aren't the spiritually inclined communities of our civilization supposed to set the example here?

You bet we are. So let us indeed finally do our part, and know that God and our planet will love us and bless us as we do our share.

What kinds of guilt do <u>you</u> have to let go of? Are you ready to start working on this? Make some notes on how you are going to do it.

CHAPTER 22

ANGER AS A GUIDE INTO THE LAND OF HARDSHIP

We all know that anger is not a very enjoyable emotion to hold inside us. Nonetheless, we have all had extensive experience in being angry. Apparently, anger is built quite strongly into the natural package of responses that occur in both animal and human life. As our cat, who just gave birth to 5 little ones will respond angrily when anybody's action might endanger her offspring, we too will respond with anger when anyone acts in a manner which is threatening to us in any way.

This simple, natural angry response aims at creating a reaction of fear, whether it be fear of attack or just fear of loss of love; we hope in doing so to stop the action that caused our angry response. At this point you may ask is this kind of anger always bad or wrong? Obviously not! Nature has with good reason built this protective or self-protective mechanism into us. Problems arise, however, when we have difficulty returning from our angry response-state back to our state of relaxation and enjoyment of life. When this happens, we set up a resonance between our emotional energy and our environment which we can expect not to be enjoyable.

Let me give some examples here:

Juliette, a single woman, 35 years old, came for counseling. Her main challenge in life appeared to be that she was always angry, and she did not like the way her life was evolving. She was the youngest of three sisters. Her father, who wanted sons, did not hide his disappointment that his last child was again the wrong gender; Juliette could never gain his appreciation. When she was 13, the husband of her eldest sister started sexually abusing her. As this man and her father were the main male figures in her life, she started hating all men. And as we always receive from our physical world what we believe in our inner world to be the truth, the men with whom she had relationships in her adult life were also, without exception, abusive toward her. Juliette had been successful as an editor of a magazine until about a year before she came to me, when she was fired. She had not been able to find work since that time, and her anger had just kept growing. So we began to work on her limited belief system about men. In helping her to realize that she had had many incarnations as a male herself, I was able to help her shift into the a better understanding of the nature of men, which helped her to draw much different and better relationships into her life. She also saw that in generating and radiating such strong angry energy into her world, she was making it very difficult for herself to receive cooperation and support from it, as the laws of sowing and reaping still determine the resonances that we create for ourselves.

An example from my own experience: many years ago now, in 1992, my father-in-law, who had come to Arizona a year before, passed away very suddenly, at 89 years of age. Apparently he had developed some kind of silent symptomless pneumonia following a cold. Within a matter of hours he became progressively worse, so quickly that the ambulance called to take him to the hospital found him already dead. Since our family physician, who had planned to see him later that day had not yet arrived, a police investigation was begun to determine if he died from natural causes or not. My late wife Joan and I were questioned very harshly for almost four hours and insinuations were made that we had let him die in total neglect to collect his inheritance. I do not recall ever having been more angry as a result of this kind of accusation. Most of that night I lay awake planning to take our accusers to the highest court if necessary to prove our innocence. Not until the evening of the next day did I calm down sufficiently to receive some inner guidance that was telling me that now I was not practicing what I preached! If I truly wanted a court battle I could have one by continuing to generate a battle with my angry thoughts. However by realizing that we had done nothing wrong and that we were not in need of any kind of punishment, I could also totally stop energizing this conflict by not even thinking about it any more. I discussed this insight with Joan and we both managed to step out of our angry attitudes and not give the matter any more thought. Several weeks later, we received a phone call from the senior homicide detective at the local police department. He asked for some additional information as he could not make sense out of the initial police report. Within a few days all accusations were withdrawn and our names were totally cleared.

This was a rather powerful demonstration of the laws of physical manifestation for both Joan and myself. I am quite sure that if we had not changed our attitude when we did we would have generated a court battle through our own anger. Apparently after some 24 hours of generating court battle thoughts, we were still able to cancel that energy and prevent the actual event.

In summary, we will have to live with the presence of anger in our lives a while longer. But let us try to limit our angry responses to short-lived reactions that are protective or educational in nature, and refrain from long-term anger, understanding that the consequences of sending out angry thought forms into our world creates trouble. Thought creates! So let us create what we really want! And if we do not want hardship and battle, then we need to stop right now energizing that type of creative manifestation. Begin to enjoy the shift in responses from your world that you will create when you monitor your creative thought and feeling energy! For your effort God will bless you; and our planet, overburdened as it is with human anger, will thank you very much.

How do you plan to get out of <u>your</u> land of hardship? Try to observe yourself when you get angry, and work diligently to learn to release that anger as fast as you can.

CHAPTER 23

HOW INNOCENT ARE BABIES?

The expression "as innocent as a baby" is widely used and speaks to everyone's imagination. How could there be anything but innocence and purity in that little pink piece of divine magic that can already smile? And consequently, when anything happens to a baby that is not very nice, like acts of aggression, neglect or abuse, we are inclined to direct great anger and possible violence toward the ones who commit those acts.

We all tend to resonate with these attitudes; and yet this implies that we have at least two blind spots in our ability to apply the spiritual teachings we have supposedly absorbed:

1. When we accept the principle of reincarnation as a truth, we must then also be willing to see that into that sweet little baby's body a soul may have landed that planned to balance a lot of negative

actions from the past in this lifetime, and that it wants to start right away. This often means going through the same negative experiences that it had inflicted upon others before.

2. We must also try to apply the understanding that, as human souls and co-creators with God, we have been given the divine gift of free choice as a learning tool; therefore we are responsible for any and all life circumstances we find ourselves in at any time. But when does this start to apply? When we are old enough to vote? Or as soon as we are born?

We have to face the fact that to this day God is receiving a lot of blame from people, even from spiritual seekers, for the terrible things He from time to time seemingly allows to happen to babies. This is a definite blind spot on our part, for it does not allow us to see that even God cannot revoke His gift of free will to us; He allows us to seek out those life experiences that are most meaningful for us to learn from, or to balance the negative actions we inflicted upon others in the past, even if we choose to start working on those issues right away after our arrival in this earth plane.

For example: Danielle, a very nice, loving, caring young lady I was counseling was trying to overcome her very difficult childhood. As a daughter of an alcoholic, abusive and aggressive father, and a mother who had totally withdrawn, doing just the necessary work and unable to give any love or nurturing because she had totally shut down from a sense of feeling defeated, Danielle grew up with a sense of never being good enough to even deserve love or attention. The result was a total lack of self-confidence and even being uncomfortable receiving physical expressions of affection in her adult life.

In a regression, having been asked to be connected with the life that created the scenario for this lifetime, she saw herself once again as the daughter of two alcoholic parents, who were aggressive and violent and showed a total absence of love and nurturing for her. It appeared that this was not the real cause of this cycle of difficult lifetimes. Asking again to be connected to the lifetime that led to this one, she now saw herself as a young, single mother under very difficult circumstances with a baby that never stopped screaming. At one point, totally exhausted and frustrated, in a fit of anger, she smothered her baby to death. Tremendous guilt followed and she ended that lifetime in total hopelessness with the belief that she would never again deserve any love or nurturing from anyone.

So now we can see how it makes sense that she drew those subsequent difficult life experiences to herself. Apparently, the atonement she made in the first past life that she remembered was not enough; she wanted or created even more suffering at the beginning of this present lifetime.

Connecting with these insights has greatly helped Danielle to get out of blaming her parents in this life for what happened and she has made great progress in overcoming these issues.

So, once again, how innocent and how helpless are babies really? Would it not help us to realize more than we have, that a sweet little baby's body can be the dwelling place for a tormented soul, who feels that a sweet happy childhood could not in any way meet his needs? And also to realize that to blame God for allowing a difficult childhood to happen is totally meaningless?

It is now time for us all to become very clear and to eliminate as many limiting belief systems as we can, as our part of the tremendous "homework" that our human family has to do at these crossroads in time, where we are meant to enter a new "chapter in the book" of our human evolution. In this new chapter, there will no longer be a place for judgment, blame, or resentment, not even for blind spots in our spiritual understanding, all of which are still limiting our capacity to expand to a higher level of self-realization and a better relationship with God.

Some more room to reflect upon the judgments and blame you have carried about events which inevitably have ramifications that you cannot yet fully understand.

CHAPTER 24

ON SOWING, REAPING AND SLOW MIRRORS

About two thousand years ago we were given a number of powerful spiritual teachings out of which I would like to address these two:

1) As you sow, so shall you reap.
2) Do unto others as you would have them do unto you.

We might say here that the second teaching appears to encourage us to apply the first one to our life.

So after all this time, how well are we doing in applying these teachings in our human family interactions? As we look at the great majority of human interactions, we have to conclude that most people must not believe these teachings to be true, in spite of the countless sermons, preached in a great variety of Christian churches each

Sunday morning, in which these principles have been taught.

It appears that we have a much stronger faith that we can have our own needs met in any unscrupulous way that we choose, whether or not other people or our planet are hurt in the process.

Why is it so difficult to understand that the cosmic laws expressed in these teachings work with the vibrational resonances that we ourselves set up? And as this is the moment where every speaker or writer on this subject brings up the example of the pebble thrown in the water creating circles that go out and come back, I will do that too.

Maybe when we see people who seem to have been very successful in working themselves up to quite powerful positions with complete neglect of these teachings, we think that if they can do it we can do it too! However, if we apply the law of reincarnation to these contemplations, we have to realize that it is totally impossible for us or anyone else to judge who gets away with what and who does not. Trust me on this. Cosmic laws never fail to be effective. So we had better prepare ourselves to fall into any hole we have dug for another person.

Maybe our difficulty in understanding these teachings is related to the fact that any amount of time can pass between the moment we create a cause and when the effect comes back to us –– it is not an immediate effect like the ripples on the surface of a swimming pool.

There is a third teaching that emphasizes this aspect. It says that the world around us acts like a mirror –– what we radiate out into the world is mirrored back to us. However, this is not a normal mirror, but is a slow, time-delayed mirror which reserves the right to decide when it will give us a reflection. Imagine standing in front of a mirror and having to wait for your reflection to appear? This does not fit our collective need at this time for instant gratification. And yet, this is how the cosmic laws operate. While we do not have time nor patience they do; and they will find the most suitable moment for either honoring the way in which we honored them by sending out ripples of love and caring, or they will get back at us, by reflecting the lack of love and caring that we expressed.

Understanding this mechanism is extremely helpful in the process of learning to stop blaming other people or God for the reflections in the mirror of our world that we do not like. We can safely assume that we ourselves and no one else have set ourselves up for this learning experience, so we had better make the best of it now, without creating more negative resonances as we would do by blaming others.

In testing these laws consciously have we not learned that Jesus knew what he was talking about and that they do indeed work? So let us then use these insights to become very determined now only to send out into our world (mirrors) the energy patterns that we want to be reflected back to us. Let us finally assume responsibility for our co-creatorship with God and stop adding any more to the already overwhelmingly large reservoirs of negativity that we have created in the past out of our ignorance or stubbornness. The universe will obviously be grateful to us for our efforts in applying these spiritual laws as they are so desperately needed at this time. So let us stay with it!

Room for some notes on how <u>you</u> can change the response of the world to your attitudes.

CHAPTER 25

ON THE TREE OF KNOWLEDGE AND HOW TO GET BACK TO THE GARDEN

When we have had one of those stressful days, or even weeks, we may wonder why it is that we have to function in this world of suffering, and work and eat our food "by the sweat of our brow."

Why did God set us up with the Tree of Knowledge of Good and Evil and the serpent when we, or our two primary ancestors, were still in that wonderful Garden of Eden? Why did He put that tree there in the first place? We would have been just fine there with the Tree of Life and still be able to enjoy the beauty, the harmony, and the balance of that special sheltered environment! Maybe we were meant to work through a learning period, wrestling with man's knowledge, eventually to rise above its inherent limitations and then return to applying Divine Knowledge to our life.

This was explained in a simple, yet profound teaching I attended, given by Rabbi Michael Shapiro. He said when Adam and Eve ate from the Tree of Knowledge of Good and Evil they became aware of Good and Evil, which is like good and bad, right and wrong. It was through the act of absorbing that energy that they entered a world of greater density, of more limitations and illusions — the world of judgment. And God's warning given earlier about the Tree of Knowledge, that "in the day thou eatest thereof thou shalt surely die" (Gen.2:17) becomes more meaningful when we understand that dying here is to be interpreted as having to move down into greater density. After all, God knew that He created us as immortal beings.

So here we are, in our current earthly environment that apparently had to be created for us when we needed it to learn to work through our world of judgment. For Adam and Eve, before they ate the forbidden fruit, there was no good or bad, as everything was in harmony and balance. The only discernment they had to make in that dimension was the one between true and false, relating to the state of affairs in what is called the astral plane of existence in our spiritual studies.

Is this indeed a fruit we will enjoy eating? True or false? We will find out the moment we eat it. This discernment separates the real from the unreal, which is of a higher order than the discernment between good and bad, which is so often, if not always, based upon illusionary perceptions. So maybe the story of the Garden is mainly a symbolic representation of the higher astral world where we dwelled until it was time to dive down into the harsh physical reality of the third dimension, and consequently into suffering; our earth school of learning. So what hope is offered by these insights? Do they offer us a key to open up the Garden again or to persuade the cherubim at the Gates to let us back through?

Of course! All we have to do to be allowed back in is to give up our judgments! So, just simply obeying the Divine commandment not to judge can indeed accomplish a transformation of our world back into an earthly paradise. How simple and yet how difficult. We are, through our many incarnations in this earth plane, totally soaked and saturated with judgments about everything and everyone, including ourselves. We are finally becoming aware in the holistic health arena how damaging this attitude has been and still is to our mental, emotional and physical state of health, as was explained in chapter 20.

Does this provide any motivation to move away, or rise above the energy or the world of judgment? I sincerely hope so, as our world reflects clearly enough the need for such a collective human initiative. If we just start by monitoring our thought processes and catch ourselves when we engage in making a judgment, we can change our attitude in that moment to one of allowing that person or that situation to be imperfect, as we are all still imperfect; and also allow everyone in each situation, including ourselves, to learn and grow in our own way, to make our own mistakes, thus no longer shutting down our love for those other persons or ourselves as we always do when we judge. In this way we restore love as the primary interaction as it is meant to be in our world, or even our universe, and in doing so we will uplift our planet with us, finding ourselves before we know it back in the Garden of Eden. So let us start today to work toward this ideal! Let us switch our mind monitors on and reset those dials from judging to allowing! I will see you later in the Garden!

Make a list of <u>your</u> judgments which you have not yet been able or willing to let go of, and reflect on how this delays our collective return to the Garden.

CHAPTER 26

ON MAN AS A DIVINE
ANSWERING SERVICE

Since ancient times our spiritual leaders have always stressed that we should help the poor and feed the hungry. This would not just help them but would also help us to maintain and strengthen the divine flow of abundance and prosperity coming our way.

Today the local poor and hungry people often present themselves at major street intersections in our cities with cardboard signs stating that they are homeless, out of work, with a family and willing to work for food.

So how do we deal with them? Is what we hear true that they will just use the money we give them to buy drugs or booze? Is it true that they can make up to $300 a day just standing on that street corner? And that they are not really serious about accepting work for food? Or are there also people among them who are really down and out and do seriously need our support in this moment?

While our mind would like to follow the strategy that we have created for ourselves or a set of rules to either give or not give depending upon certain outer characteristics of the people with these cardboard signs, this would probably not lead to a maximum effectiveness in our charity efforts.

What would be a better course of action? Let me explain what I have learned on my journey here. In my present understanding, when people in their desperation pray to God for help, God likes to answer them through actions of other people who are, for the moment, promoted to being a divine instrument and who do not necessarily need to be aware of this in order for God's answer to be effective. This mechanism is used in many areas of need not just with food. Let me give a personal example in the story of Gina.

My late wife Joan has done many spiritual readings for people. Through her gift of clairaudience, she could hear answers to questions of a spiritual nature, mainly focusing on solving personal problems. She would then write them down and present the answer.

Sometimes she would get spontaneous messages like in this case. One morning, she awoke at 7 a.m. and felt there was a message to write down. She wrote a whole page, then called me and said, "Isn't this strange? I wrote a whole page starting with Dear Gina. I don't know any Gina! What am I to do with this?" I thought for a moment and said, "Wait a minute! I know a Gina! I met her a few weeks ago. Let me call her and check if this message makes any sense to her." So I did. I called her on the phone, explained the situation and read the message.

Gina was in tears. She explained to me how in total desperation she had prayed to God the night before asking for a sign, a message about whether or not she should continue to put energy into her ailing business.

So now I was really impressed. Look at the profound mechanism at work here. Gina prays to God. God directs the response to the local "upstairs" management, which realizes that Gina in her turmoil would not hear His answer, but knows that through Joan and her husband the answering circuit could be completed. So here we were, blessed with the opportunity to be part of a divine answering service.

Now back to our poor and hungry. When we approach an intersection with a cardboard sign person, the key is not to think, but feel in our heart what we are asked to do here and sometimes we will feel the urge to give. But sometimes that urge does not appear so clearly. Apparently, when the urge to give is there we are in the divine response circuitry; if we do not feel it we probably are not. Perhaps when that happens we are sensing that they are one of those who do not really need our help, and who did not ask God for any either. But surely God will find another human instrument who can help them when the time is right –– when they are ready to receive and positively respond to that help.

So there are no rules other than we should feel what we are asked to do, rather than thinking ourselves into hardening our hearts for the wrong reasons, or giving out of guilt when we are not asked to do so at that particular time.

If we can all practice this type of attunement to the divine needs and wishes whenever we can, we will create a better world.

Plan here to ask for God's specific guidance on how <u>you</u> can become a better divine instrument than you already are.

CHAPTER 27

ON THE HUMAN BODY AS GOD'S IMAGE AND LIKENESS

In counseling cancer patients, I often find that their illness is the first opportunity they have had in their life to shift from their perception that their body is like some kind of a machine that can have something wrong with it, to the realization that instead their body is a rather miraculous expression of the complexity of their personality's energy patterns, whether they are beautiful and harmonious, creating radiant health and strength, or filled with pain, grief, anger and bitterness expressing these disharmonies in the form of this illness.

In my experience, a requirement to overcome cancer is the ability to make this shift, to start taking responsibility for that which we create through our thoughts and feelings; to stop blaming others and God for what is wrong with our life or our body, and instead start practicing our spiritual knowledge, remembering that we are indeed made in God's image and likeness and are co-creators with Him.

A common error we make in our efforts to understand that we are made in God's image and likeness is that we try to reduce God to a human form —— the big old guy with a white beard, sitting on His throne, judging and punishing all of us who do not obey his commands. This is a sadly limiting concept and far from the truth. Why do we not start to acknowledge that the human mind cannot understand and define God, just as a 3 year old cannot yet understand complex mathematical equations?

Let me give an example here to illustrate this. We all know about the striking similarity between an atom and our solar system. We say "as above, so below," but let us take this one step further. Let us suppose for a moment that the countless billions of atoms in our body are like little suns, and the electrons, circling around the nuclei, as little planets? And also suppose that there are minute tiny life forms, little people living on those planets inside of us?

Our present scientific methods have no way of proving this to be either true or false. The statement "as above, so below" suggests that it might very well be true, as do other spiritual teachings. Quite a fascinating idea is it not? Very helpful in shifting our perception to seeing our body no longer as a solid bag of flesh and bones but mostly made up of space, the true solid matter of which could easily fit onto a pinhead if the space around the atom nuclei (suns) and electrons (planets) were eliminated. So we are more like a human energy field held together by our consciousness than anything else.

Now let us go back for a moment to the little people living on those planets (electrons) in our body. Let us suppose that somewhere inside us these little people are trying to understand and define God. Can we ask or even demand from them that they be able to recognize or even imagine you? Obviously not. And yet, you are very much like God to them; in you they live, move and have their being. Imagine what happens to them when you get angry. Powerful magnetic storms, possibly hurricanes and earthquakes shake up their little world. Quite a responsibility for us! And imagine how they will feel when we are truly in love with life, with our God and ourselves, and all those worlds inside us —— what great healing and what divine revelations will happen to them! How blessed they will feel!

Let us now apply the "as above, so below" in the other direction. Perhaps our solar system is just an atom in the body of God? Quite a humbling thought is it not? Just a moment ago we realized how extremely powerful and mighty we must seem to those myriads of worlds inside of us. And now we are back to realizing that we are just like them.

Obviously we can easily get lost in these concepts. But I find them extremely helpful in reminding us that our mind will not yet be able for quite some time in our human evolution to truly understand the vastness of the Divine Mind.

What we can see now, however, is that keeping our mind in harmony and balance is vitally important in even more ways than we ever before realized. Because we need to serve through the creative power of our thoughts, the worlds above as well as the worlds below or inside of us, keeping our mind and body healthy now takes on a whole new meaning.

So, be well! May God bless you in your efforts to connect and resonate with the Divine Love which has made all these worlds go 'round since the beginning of time.

Room for your thoughts on how you're growing understanding of the vastness of God's Universe is helping you to expand your outlook on life.

CHAPTER 28

THE GARDEN OF EDEN AS A WORKPLACE

Recently I read that the average personal debt of an adult American citizen is about $20,000. Some people are so acutely aware of this that they drive to work in the morning with bumper stickers on their cars that say, "I owe, I owe, so off to work I go!" They may even daydream about how nice it would be to be back in the Garden of Eden where they would be provided with everything they would need without the need for money, with no risk of debt and without the need to work as we do here in this third dimensional world "by-the-sweat-of-our-brow." Is it possible to bridge the gap between these two worlds in our attitude toward work? It should be, if the title of this chapter is to make any sense. Let us look into this further.

In our spiritual studies, we find that the Garden of Eden symbolically represents the astral world, where we lived in total harmony with our environment. This was facilitated by the fact that in that world we were not involved in the duality, the world of good and bad, right and wrong, in other words, the world of judgment we live in now, as was explained in Chapter 25. Is it possible that we were cast out of the Garden into this world not so much as a punishment, but rather as a new episode in our learning and growth, to explore this realm and integrate it into our total awareness? Where before we could meet our needs in the astral world through desire, we could manifest in front of us what we needed, here we feel that manifestation of what we need, such as money, requires hard work in the physical realm, the dimension of action.

Let me give you an example: a new real estate licensee learns in the broker's office "the ropes" of the job. In order to be successful, he or she is told it is necessary to make 100 cold telephone calls in the morning and knock on an equal number of doors in the afternoon to motivate people to buy or sell a home. In addition the new licensee is told to set monthly and annual goals of how much money is to be generated.

The first part of this instruction obviously represents the 3rd-dimensional, sweat-of-our-brow attitude about work and how to create what we need. Yet, is it not fascinating to realize that the second part, the goal-setting, which preferably is to be written down and thought about a lot, is actually the Garden of Eden way of manifesting through conscious desire by holding a thought in our mind until it is manifested in our present reality as physical form? It is as if we still remember how we created what we needed the easy way, but we do not trust that mechanism enough and, therefore, engage in all this action of phone calls and door-to-door visits.

There are many prosperity seminars given in this country every weekend where people are taught, or rather reminded, that even today in this world of ours things do not need to be so difficult and laborious. E.g., the real estate licensee, who is aware of this will decide to sit quietly in meditation every morning, visualizing people who need to buy or sell a home connecting with him or her spontaneously. This person will also, on the side, work on affirming his or her worthiness to receive abundance and prosperity in this way without generating guilt over making all this money without pushing telephone buttons and door bells every day.

So, basically, we need to realize or remember that we have always remained co-creators with God throughout our travels through this universe, and that it is perfectly appropriate to use the mental and emotional avenues of creative manifestation in this physical realm. Relying primarily on physical work activity to create is, in a way, like putting the cart before the horse. As many of us are realizing, it is now time to pull ourselves out of the density of the belief system that physical action is the primary requirement for creative manifestation.

Let us now rely much more than we have before on our gut feeling, our intuitive nature, in our work attitude. Let us ask to be connected with those people who we can help and who can help us to realize our goals, financial or otherwise, all in a playful, spontaneous manner, reducing if not removing the sweat-of-our-brow idea of work entirely. In this way we can indeed regain the Garden of Eden as a state of being and make it our workplace in the true spirit of Kahlil Gibran's definition, "Work is love made visible."

CHAPTER 29

MEDITATION -- THE FAST LANE TO ENLIGHTENMENT

Why Do We Need to Meditate?

As a reader of this book, I trust you are 1) already practicing meditation daily, or 2) contemplating to do so, or perhaps 3) have tried and found that it was not working and stopped. This chapter is designed for those of you in categories 2 and 3 to help you get started or try again.

Why can we not live a good life of service and grow spiritually without meditation? We can but it would be like taking the slow road compared to what we can accomplish with regular, daily meditation. Let me explain.

We have all lived many lives of imperfection on this planet and possibly others, exploring and gathering experience in realms where love does not reign. We have learned very much there, enough so that we can now try to stay on the path of righteousness, love and compassion.

However, our subconscious mind is carrying a big Pandora's box of unresolved, unhealed old memories of suffering, either as physical pain, rejection and abandonment, abuse, or any other variation on the theme of lack of the love and nurturing we have always needed. Each one of these old unresolved issues can become a trigger for disharmonious behavior expressed as fear, anger, or just distress. We rarely, if ever, become angry or upset because the situation we are currently facing calls for a response of anger or distress. At that moment, we shift from a conscious mind-response to a subconscious mind-response, allowing that part of our being, which largely operates outside our conscious control, to take over for a moment and release a small part of its vast reservoir of repressed, disharmonious energy. This energy is activated because the present issue triggers a deep memory of our old difficulties with similar issues. So, while we never plan to get angry or upset we do, nonetheless, because we do not have enough control over our subconscious mind to prevent it from jumping in. After a while, when we calm down, our conscious mind is back in charge.

How can we rise above this rather limited way of responding to the challenges and opportunities of life? We can of course go to psychotherapists or counselors who will, if they are good, assist us in reconnecting with those old issues through various therapeutic systems and techniques and help us with the clearing and healing we need. Or we can take an active role. What we can do for ourselves is limited to only two levels of action: dreaming and meditation. Dreaming is our subconscious mind's natural attempt to process and overcome traumatic events. For example: If a 4 year old child has to undergo a tonsillectomy and is not prepared for the experience in an honest manner, the child can experience the event as a very frightening type of punishment, creating a state of shock and basic insecurity about what can happen in this world. Almost immediately, the child will start dreaming about this experience over and over again until it loses its fearfulness, which can take months or even years. When these dreams stop the child has completed the processing.

Compared to dreaming, meditation is a far superior method of clearing the subconscious mind of its traumatic issues. It is helpful here to realize that our subconscious mind is always trying to release its issues, but it cannot get our attention except through the trigger mechanisms of our uncontrolled emotional responses because we keep our conscious mind constantly busy with all of our daily activities. Only when we stop the activity of our conscious mind, which is the main focus in meditation, can our subconscious mind let its contents rise, like little air bubbles through water, to our conscious awareness, in the form of thoughts and feelings, rising up to the calm and clear surface that we have created.

I want to emphasize how essential meditation is for the acceleration of our spiritual growth. There is yet another important aspect to this. We all want to strengthen our intuitive awareness and our ability to draw inspirational guidance from higher dimensional realms. We can only accomplish this effectively if we work at clearing the contents of our subconscious mind as we need to pass through this layer of our being to access the higher realms. In other words, we can and will be like true masters as soon as we have totally emptied our Pandora's box of its contents. To accomplish this with just our processing technique of dreaming would take many more lifetimes. Of course, we can move faster with the help of therapists, but the daily practice of meditation truly unlocks the potential of accomplishing this in our current lifetime. Let us not underestimate how much more we can contribute to the raising of the consciousness of the human family by giving time for meditation priority in our daily lives. God, the angels and the entire Brotherhood of Light will breathe a big sigh of relief when we finally get to it. So get ready!

CHAPTER 30

MEDITATION: THE FAST LANE TO ENLIGHTENMENT

How To Practice

In the previous chapter, I made an effort to explain that meditation is such an important tool to accelerate our spiritual growth and stay centered in this close to crazy world of our time that we simply cannot afford not to practice it.

So how do we practice meditation? Can we just sit down, close our eyes and ears to the world and order our mind not to think? We could try, but most likely if that were to be our first attempt, it would not work and we would simply get very frustrated and find out that our mind does not want to be shut off. It finds many sneaky ways every minute to get us back to thinking about our ongoing worries or whatever else arises.

Here are some helpful suggestions we can follow to be more successful:

1. Reserve a special time when it is quiet, such as early morning or later in the evening when the telephone, doorbell and the kids are hopefully quiet.

2. Create a special quiet and peaceful place in your home to practice meditation where you will, through your practice, generate a quiet and peaceful energy that will eventually, when strong enough, facilitate your efforts to enter the stillness. You may want to have some special objects there such as a picture of a source of spiritual inspiration for you, some holy books, crystals, etc., which all work toward the desired effect.

3. Be determined to succeed and realize that you will be bombarded by mental as well as physical distractions (itches, aches, etc.) that may suggest to you that this will never work.

4. Sit down quietly in comfortable clothing. Start by energizing your body and clearing your mind using any of the intensified breathing techniques that are available. If you know one that works for you, stay with that for a few minutes. A technique that I picked up from my meditation teacher, Michael Shapiro, goes as follows: Breathe in for a count of 4, using abdominal breathing and pushing your navel forward. Hold for a count of 8. Then still holding the breath, bring the navel

backward as close to the spinal column as you can, tightening the anal muscles, and hold for another 8 counts. Then exhale for a count of 4 and repeat.

After some 12 cycles of this your body is nicely energized or charged, and you will find that it is easier now to keep your mind quieter than before. For some people, practicing physical (yoga) exercises before starting to meditate has a similar beneficial effect.

We can now enter the meditative state. But it would be too dangerous to let our mind roam free. So we give it a very simple focusing task to do, like repeating a mantra (if we know one that feels good, one we preferably received through our own inner guidance), or by simply observing our breath going in and out without controlling it as if we were observing someone else's breathing. As we do this, distracting thoughts will still arise. Do not get caught, frustrated or angry, but simply observe the thought in a detached manner, mentally opening the door to let it leave and return to observing the breath. With practice, the times of stillness in between the thoughts will increase and so will your satisfaction with the sense of relaxation and centeredness that you will experience.

How long do we need to meditate? And how often? We have to realize here that while even five minutes spent in meditation is beneficial, the real benefits come with daily practice, if possible a half hour to an hour. It is in the second half hour that we find ourselves quiet enough to have the subconscious mind's issues, the old repressed unhappy memories, surface to our awareness which we can then observe in a detached manner and release them.

Do not get emotionally involved again; that only adds strength to the repressed energy of that issue. Our old issues, those buttons that get pushed and trigger sudden disharmonious behavior, like angry or jealous outbursts, will gradually diminish in strength and, with continued practice of meditation, gradually fade out. We are left with a beautiful sense of clarity, harmony and a much stronger ability to receive intuitive and inspirational guidance, which will help to lift us above and beyond patterns of denial of love toward ourselves and others that have kept us moving in circuits of limitation for many lifetimes.

So meditation will, in this way, greatly strengthen the light and energy that we carry with us as well as help us to remember that we always were great spiritual light beings, that have, through our long series of earthly incarnations, become so caught up in the density of this third dimension, that we have forgotten who we really are. It is time to remember who we truly are! Our planet needs us to do so, as does the spiritual hierarchy that is working so hard to guide us through this planetary hour of initiation.

A word of caution. Do not do the breathing exercise as given above while driving a car. The altered state, induced by its powerful effects, may impair your driving ability. Also, realize that practicing meditation will increase your light, i.e. your energy and what we may call your personal power and impact on other people. This means that when you feel good and balanced, people will feel better than before in your presence. It also means that when you get angry, much more power than before is channeled into that anger with the potential for greater destructive consequences.

As the driver of a car with a small 4-cylinder engine needs to learn how to handle his car once a big V-8 engine is built into it, so will you need to learn to properly handle and enjoy the greater powers that become available to you through the practice of meditation. As spiritual power is magnified many times when a group of people meditate together, it is very helpful to strive to do this preferably once a week or even more often, as this can provide yet another means to accelerate your progress.

So, now you have enough tools to get started. Know that God is with you in this endeavor and good luck!